ADDICTION
A HUMAN EXPERIENCE

Third Edition

Rowena Ramnath, Psy.D.
William Berry, LMHC, CAP

SAN DIEGO

Bassim Hamadeh, CEO and Publisher
Carrie Montoya, Manager, Revisions and Author Care
Kaela Martin, Project Editor
Abbey Hastings, Associate Production Editor
Jess Estrella, Senior Graphic Designer
Alexa Lucido, Licensing Supervisor
Natalie Piccotti, Senior Marketing Manager
Kassie Graves, Vice President of Editorial
Jamie Giganti, Director of Academic Publishing

Cover image taken by Alexi Berry.

Printed in the United States of America.

www.cognella.com   800-200-3908

CONTENTS

Preface

The intention of this book is to foster a greater awareness of those who develop a substance use problem and the experience of treating these individuals. The idea is to provide a basic overview of the addiction experience, with a focus on what the experience is like for the addicted person.

This book will serve as an adjunct to other addiction textbooks already used in psychology courses addressing pathological substance use; it does not focus on the interaction of drugs with the body or the brain, the history of substances, or the medical consequences of substance use. Instead, the emphasis is on theories of why people become addicted, the counselor's role in helping, how addiction affects thinking, the family's role when a member becomes addicted, the typical recovery process, and the typical relapse process. Other topics focus on relationships, spirituality, and co-occurring disorders in addiction recovery, as well as harm reduction and relapse prevention. Moreover, this third edition is compatible with the *Diagnostic and Statistical Manual of Mental Disorders-Fifth Edition (DSM-5)*. There has been a significant classification and taxonomic shift in the *DSM-5* concerning addiction, and the authors have been inclusive of those changes. The reader is encouraged to explore the *DSM-5* in addition to reading this text for a more comprehensive understanding of the changes.

The two most significant ideas the authors seek to impart are fostering understanding and compassion for those seeking treatment for addiction, and providing basic treatment approaches. With this intent in mind, it is also the authors' contention that there can be no one-size-fits-all treatment for substance use or addiction; all individuals are different. Rudimentary ideas about addiction and its treatment must be tempered with a desire to understand the individual.

The information presented in this text is a reflection of your authors' combined 30 years of experience treating and researching addiction. Case examples are provided to illuminate each topic.

An enormous amount of material is available on addiction and its treatment, and much of it can be helpful to those trying to grasp this dilemma. In this text, your authors attempt not to proclaim a final conclusion that will prove successful in the treatment of addiction, but simply to make the reader aware of the experience in the field, as well as some of the leading writers on these topics.

Keeping this in mind, we hope you gain an understanding that addiction truly is a human experience.

CHAPTER ONE

Who Needs and Enters Treatment

Learning Objectives

- Understand who needs and enters substance disorder treatment.
- Explain the difference between substance use and substance-induced disorders.
- Identify bottoms and their value.
- Describe the difference between internal and external motivation.
- Understand the counselor's role in sustaining motivation.
- Identify type of treatment.
- Identify types of substance disorder assessments.

Introduction

An often long and winding road, substance disorder treatment brings many challenges and gains for both the addicted and the counselors. The field itself is rich with research and evidence-based treatment modalities that have proven to be efficacious, given the right conditions. However, the nature of the addiction, the individual's life circumstances, the motivational level, and the quality of the intervention are all factors that are interdependent on each other for a successful outcome. Many individuals who suffer from addiction do not feel they need treatment. Conversely, many do realize they need treatment, but their dependence on the substance is so great that they cannot enter treatment volitionally. Oftentimes it takes a legal, personal, or financial consequence that is extreme in nature to drive a person to enter treatment. There are many cases in which drug treatment is a mandated alternate in a correctional setting, forcing intervention and access to recovery. Ultimately, to truly understand who needs and enters treatment, one must fully grasp what addiction means and what types of treatment are available.

DSM-5

When working with the addiction population, it is important to fully understand the terminology used to describe the varying degrees of alcohol, drug, medication, and toxin consumption. The *Diagnostic and Statistical Manual of Mental Disorders, Fifth Edition* (DSM-5), is the cornerstone for describing and diagnosing the use of these substances. A person is only diagnosed if they report experiencing clinical symptomatology. Therefore, ingesting alcohol, toxins, medications, or drugs on a casual/social basis without experiencing negative consequences does not warrant a diagnosis. Moreover, the mental health field has moved away from the once-used terms *substance abuse* and *substance dependence* and embraced a new taxonomy with a slight shift in understanding. The following is an overview of recent changes. A detailed explanation of the DSM-5 is beyond the scope of this book, although highly encouraged by the authors.

In 2013, the DSM-5 introduced "Substance-Related and Addictive Disorders," which are reflective of the brain's reward system of repeated stimulation that results in brain circuit changes. The substances recognized by the DSM-5 as having the capacity to induce these brain changes that can lead to disordered use are alcohol, caffeine, cannabis, hallucinogens, inhalants, opioids, sedatives, hypnotics and anxiolytics, stimulants, tobacco, and others. Each substance now has its own diagnostic criteria with specifiers and severity indicators. Among the substance-related disorders are two groups: **substance use disorders** and **substance-induced disorders**.

Substance Use Disorders

Of the 10 substances mentioned above, all with the exception of caffeine can be classified as a substance use disorder due to pathological behavioral patterns. Each disorder is organized into groupings with set criteria. The first general group is **impaired control**. This describes increased use over an unintended length of time; a desire to stop with unsuccessful attempts; a significant proportion of time dedicated toward acquiring, using, and recovering from the substance; and cravings. **Social impairment**, the second grouping, is a failure to fulfill major duties at work, school, or home; using the substance despite persistent or recurrent social or interpersonal problems; and important social, occupational, or recreational activities decrease or stop because of use. The third grouping of criteria for substance use disorders is **risky use**. This reflects continued use irrespective of troubles caused by physical hazards, or continued use despite knowledge of having a persistent or recurrent psychological problem. The last grouping describes **pharmacological criteria**: tolerance and withdrawal. **Tolerance** is the increased consumption in order to achieve the same desired effect. **Withdrawal** indicates the physiological results of a decreased concentration of the substance in the blood or tissue of the individual. Both tolerance and withdrawal vary greatly from individual to specific substance. The experience of tolerance and withdrawal while a person is using prescribed medications for a specific treatment is not considered to be a substance use disorder. These are general criteria, and in the DSM-5, each category of substance has the criteria individualized. It is necessary to consult the DSM-5 to make an accurate diagnosis.

Severity and Specifiers

Once a person has been diagnosed with a substance use disorder, it is expected of the clinician to indicate severity. "Mild" suggests the presence of two or three symptoms. "Moderate" indicates four or five symptoms. "Severe" would be a person who demonstrates six or more symptoms. Evidently, the severity of symptoms can fluctuate over time. Therefore, it is appropriate for the clinician to indicate so. Also important are the specifiers that provide context to the diagnosis. Examples of specifiers are "In Early Remission," (3 months but less than one year abstinence), "In Full Sustained Remission" (abstinent from all substances for more than a year) "On Maintenance Therapy," (on a prescribed medication to reduce craving or effects of the drug's use), or "in a controlled environment".

Substance-Induced Disorders

Substance Intoxication and Withdrawal

The hallmark of **intoxication** is the reversible experience after recent ingestion of the substance. This experience is largely attributed to the effects of the substance on the central nervous system that are separate from any preexisting medical or mental condition. Although substance intoxication occurs in those with substance use disorders, it is now a diagnosable syndrome (excluding tobacco) in the DSM-5 (American Psychiatric Association, 2013). The experience of intoxication includes disturbances in the following areas: perception, wakefulness, attention, thinking, judgment, and psychomotor and interpersonal behavior. The period of intoxication can vary depending on the specific substance and the amount consumed.

Withdrawal is a substance-specific experience, as well. Once the concentration of the substance in the individual's cells begins to decrease, it creates a physiological response (e.g., restlessness, sweating, tremors, insomnia, headaches). This response will likely cause some level of distress or impairment in important life roles and is not due to a medical or mental condition. Typically, short-acting substances have a higher likelihood of triggering withdrawal.

Substance/Medication-Induced Mental Disorder

This particular type of mental disorder is potentially severe, albeit temporary. To be diagnosed with this versus substance use disorders suggests the experience of cognitive, behavioral, and physiological symptoms that contribute to the continued use of the substance despite associated problems. Each of the 10 classes of substances may induce a mental disorder, such as depressive disorder, anxiety disorder, or neurocognitive disorder. In order to distinguish from a preexisting mental disorder, the individual's self-report and medical records must support that the disorder developed within 1 month of intoxication or withdrawal of a substance known to cause a mental disorder.

Many professionals in the field will continue to use the term **addiction** despite these recent changes in the DSM-5. Much of the typical associations with the word *addiction* are individuals who experience tolerance and withdrawal with repeated use of a given substance despite negative consequences. However, it is not necessary for a person to experience both symptoms in order to be identified as having an addiction. Moving forward, the authors will use the terms *addiction* and *substance use disorders* interchangeably to describe an individual experiencing these common signs:

- Physical dependence
- Multiple blackouts (memory loss)
- Medical complications
- Hidden use
- Dishonesty
- Conflict with loved ones over use
- DUI
- Illegal behavior (e.g., obtaining an illegal substance)
- Work problems
- Tolerance of drug of choice (increased amount of drug to attain the same effect)
- Withdrawal
- Frequent mood swings
- Irresponsibility
- Daily use

- Use while expected to fill major life responsibilities (parenting, while working, etc.)

Many who enter substance use treatment report these common symptoms. Some are forced into treatment as a result of some of these consequences. For some, these signs indicate they have hit bottom.

Bottoms

Bottom is a term commonly heard in addiction treatment and recovery. A **bottom** is when the addicted individual believes he can go no lower. He has traveled as far down in the spiral of addiction as he can go. For many, the bottom is marital strife, family discord, arrest, or physical health problems. For some, it is realized through suicidal ideation or suicide attempts. Others have what are called *high bottoms*, which denote minimal consequences, but the consequences are serious enough for this individual to seek help. For example, a woman entered treatment for alcohol use after she blacked out and bloodied her knee. As she had no recollection of the period she was awake (the definition of a blackout), she was appalled by her own behavior.

She entered treatment the next week. Of course, why a person enters treatment will vary. The most common type of bottom inciting the desire for treatment is a **low bottom**. This could be a person who has lost his or

FIGURE 1.1. When most think of addiction, they think of low bottoms: homelessness, morning use, unemployment, and illegal behavior. But many substance users are gainfully employed and are high bottoms.

her home and/or family support, is suicidal, and is experiencing severe withdrawal symptoms. Even so, those who have low bottoms often can be indifferent about getting help shortly after the crisis period has abated. Therefore, when an individual seeks treatment after a crisis that he or she believes is a low bottom, the pressure is felt by the treating clinicians, knowing that when the intervention alleviates the immediate distress, there will be a high likelihood that the motivation will wane. This is commonly experienced at detoxification centers.

DETOX CENTER

The process of an addict entering and leaving a detox center is often very contrary. This is an illustration of what that process is like: A detox center in the Northeast only accepted alcohol-dependent and heroin-addicted individuals. As they had to be in withdrawal to be admitted, they were often already physiologically uncomfortable when seeking treatment. When conducting assessments, many would beg to get in to the center because the distress they were experiencing was too overwhelming. Often heard was "I'll do anything, anything. Please just get me in." Many were admitted to the detox. You can hear in their words the desperation to stop the pain of their addiction/withdrawal. Are you surprised then that many signed out before their 3-day stay was over? Their reasoning was sometimes dramatic: "I have kids and have to get back to my job." It was sometimes more honest: "I feel much better and think I can handle it from here." And at times it was completely idiotic: "The food sucks" or "I can't believe you can't smoke here." The point is that the desperation often seen in an addict seeking treatment is generally short lived; some enter treatment with indifference or simply to appease external motivators while others are desperate for withdrawal symptom relief.

A **detox** (short for detoxification center) is usually a hospital-based program that is very short term (2 days to 1 week), where medications and support are given to help someone physically addicted to a substance free his body from the withdrawal. Substances that require medical detox are alcohol (the most dangerous to withdraw from), sedatives (such as Valium, Xanax, or barbiturates—these are often done on an outpatient basis as a result of the long duration of the symptoms), and opioids (heroin, oxycontin, roxycodone).

Whether an addict has to hit bottom or not is a topic of debate. It is often said that when people try and fail at recovery, "They did not hit bottom yet." Considering this and the high number of people who relapse after reportedly hitting their bottom, it can be supposed one will only know if he hits bottom after he remains in recovery for a significant period of time. Treatment professionals often consider it part of their job to raise the bottom for their clients so they don't have to go any lower.

Motivation

FIGURE 1.2.

When someone enters treatment, staff assesses whether the motivation is internal or external, or a combination of both. **External motivation** consists of environmental reasons to seek help or to stop substance use. These reasons include loved ones applying pressure, legal trouble that requires abstinence, licensing boards that force their members into treatment if a problem is discovered, other work or career issues, and health problems exacerbated by substance use. **Internal motivation** is the realization a behavior is detrimental to your life goals or incongruent with your values. Therefore, the drive to make a change comes from within; the decision to stop substance abuse results from this realization.

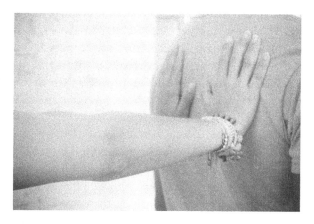

FIGURE 1.3. Consequences bring the vast majority of people into substance treatment.

Research regarding who fares better in treatment—those with internal or external motivation—suggests that the best motivation is a combination of both high internal and external motivation. Mandated treatment often assumes a high degree of external motivation; yet, it is critical for the quality of intervention provided to help foster internal motivation (Gallagher & Bremer, 2018). It is internal motivation that will increase the chances of successful recovery. In their review of the literature, DiClemente, Bellino, and Neavins (1999) purport that internal motivation is correlated with better long-term outcomes. Furthermore, studies suggest that external motivation serves the individual best in the beginning of treatment while intrinsic motivation serves the later stages of treatment and post-treatment recovery (Cannizzaro, Stohl, Hasin, & Aharonovich, 2017).

In research on outcomes for legally coerced clients, Farabee, Prendergast, and Anglin (1998) reviewed studies of coerced treatment, and although citing weaknesses, found that legally coerced treatment is at least as effective as intrinsic motivation. This supports the growth of **drug court** programs, a one-time intervention for those arrested on drug-related charges, throughout the country. Oftentimes it is avoiding jail or having driving privileges reinstated that motivates individuals to follow through with the drug court program leading to treatment exposure that can increase intrinsic motivation (Eckberg & Jones, 2015). Moreover, drug court has been demonstrated as effective in reducing recidivism rates (Cox, Brown, Hansten, & Morgan, 2001). In their review of literature and of six programs in the state of Washington, they found that besides their effectiveness in reducing recidivism, drug court programs lead to better outcomes in reduced court time and incarceration, and higher wages for graduates.

This is easy to see if one looks past what brought an individual to treatment. Those who are truly internally motivated have the desire to change their life for the better and may readily accept suggestions and go the extra mile. Those who have a monitoring system, like the courts, want to remain out of trouble by following direction. And for many externally motivated clients, it doesn't end there: They have to submit to random urine drug screens for extended periods. It is not uncommon for an individual who is court mandated to have to submit to random drug and alcohol screens, as well as involvement in a weekly monitoring group.

Although outcomes may be similar for those with strong internal motivation and those who are ordered by the court, it must be remembered that the clinician's job is to help motivate the client. Although those with low intrinsic motivation have poorer outcomes, this can be mediated to some extent through helping the client realize that any motivation can be internal. Although clients may be forced into treatment by loved ones, it is the clients' desire to please their loved ones that actually brought them in. For example, if his wife tells a client that she will leave if he doesn't go into treatment, it is the client's desire to be with his wife that brings him in. This motivation can be internalized. The focus can be on how he is making the decision rather than feeling forced into it. This allows the client to own his choice. By owning his choice, the external motivation becomes more internal.

It is important for the clinician to understand that even if the client remains unmotivated, some of the work that is being done will remain with the client and may help in the future. In the addiction field, many professionals regard their job as "planting seeds for recovery." Due to the poor outcomes for substance use, clinicians understand it may take several treatments for an individual to become abstinent in the long term. However, it may be their work early on that assists clients in recognizing their use is a problem later, and this may lead to reentering treatment.

The Counselor's Role in Sustaining Motivation

Another important area regarding motivation is sustaining motivation. As alluded to earlier, motivation for treatment and abstinence often wanes with time. This is where good counseling becomes important, as does remaining cognizant of the things that motivated treatment to begin with. It is essential that the client feel comfortable with the therapist, and it is important for the therapist to match his or her interventions to the client's stage of change.

James Prochaska and Carlo DiClemente of the University of Rhode Island developed a model describing stages of change in the early 1980s. Although this theory has face validity and has found decades of favor, some conflicting data will be presented later in Chapter 6. For now, it remains an important theory in addiction treatment.

There are six stages that an individual will move through. What is important for the counselor to recognize is that the rate at which a client moves through the stages is very individual. Often, the most difficult stage to overcome is the first stage, **precontemplation**. In this stage, the person does not even acknowledge that there is a problem. For counselors, the best form of intervention at this stage is psychoeducation (i.e., information about the effects of drugs on the body and on loved ones). Ideally, after being informed, the person will recognize that there is a problem. This is the **contemplation** stage. Counselors must be aware that, despite the person acknowledging there is a problem, the individual is not ready to make any changes in his behavior.

FIGURE 1.4. Motivational interviewing, which uses the stages of change model, is common in addiction treatment.

It is in the **preparation** stage that the person starts planning for change. Planning may include establishing a support system/support group or identifying a rehabilitation center. Once the person extinguishes the using behavior, enters rehab, or disconnects from the "using" community, she or he is considered to be in the **action** stage. This stage is typically met with the greatest motivation the client will experience. The difficulty lies in sustaining that motivation through withdrawal symptoms. One of the more challenging stages for both counselors and clients is the **maintenance** stage. This is the stage when clients will work through underlying issues that may have led to their drug/alcohol use in the first place. Although the ideal is for a person to never achieve Stage Six—**relapse**—the reality is most people will cycle back through Stages One through Five a few times before being completely abstained from substance use. Depending on the research, relapse rates of addiction range from 50% to 90%. Reasons vary why a person may relapse.

Too many times a client leaves treatment prematurely, often after only a few sessions. This happens with unfortunate regularity. There are a number of possible explanations for clients' decisions to drop out of treatment. Although the reasons to drop out are not the responsibility of the counselor, it is important for the client to find a counselor or treatment center that she or he is happy with and let the professionals help her or him maintain the motivation for treatment. The counselor and treatment facility will more likely encourage family involvement. Family can help with motivation by encouraging treatment and possibly even getting involved in the treatment process. They can remind clients of the reasons they sought treatment and provide additional motivation for the clients to remain in treatment, despite their belief they are able to discontinue.

In over 30 years of combined work in the addiction field, we can vaguely recall one or two legitimate cases where there was this type of internal motivation. In a support group where the majority of clients were impaired professionals mandated to treatment by their licensing entity, there was one gentleman who was without career or legal problems. This group member was over 50 years old and had a history of substance addiction, as well as an extended period of recovery during which he had become a paraprofessional in the field of addiction treatment. He had been battling a serious medical illness, part of which resulted in bouts of pain. Despite his legitimate benefit from pain medication, he had been taking them beyond the prescription, and admitted he took them even when not in pain. He demonstrated insight into some of the antecedents to his substance use, including his fear of his illness being terminal. However, he continued to struggle with urges for the substance despite all of his knowledge about recovery. The group members genuinely exulted his internal motivation, how great it was to have entered treatment on his own, to not be forced, and how proud he must be. When he couldn't take it anymore, he stopped them and informed them his wife made him enter the group, and that if not for her, he'd probably still be popping pain pills.

Types of Treatment

A quick overview of the types of treatment available to the substance-dependent individual is in order. When seeking treatment or determining the appropriate level of treatment for a specific client, there are a number of factors that must be considered. For example, alcohol, benzodiazepines, and opiates often require a medical intervention before or in conjunction with psychological treatment. At minimum, the individual should be evaluated to determine if he requires the medical intervention, if it needs to be inpatient or can be handled as outpatient, or if he can safely manage ceasing the substance without medication.

Generally—at least partially as a result of managed care—the substance user is placed in the minimum level of care that can safely manage his symptomatology. Considerations in determining the level of care include the client's motivation, employment, and other external responsibilities; the supportive quality (or lack thereof) of his environment; how often he uses substances, the type of substance being used; previous treatment failure and success; and what type of treatment he can afford. The level of care is determined by the evaluating counselor and must be reassessed consistently and as situations change. Often (and this is correlated with increased success), the substance user begins in one level of care and "steps down" to a less intense level of care.

Detoxification Centers

As stated above, inpatient detoxification centers are usually short term, from 2 days to 1 week. The common substances for inpatient detoxification are alcohol and opioids. Outpatient detoxification is growing in popularity for opioid use. This type of detoxification is also used for benzodiazepines, as the withdrawal may last a substantial period of time, making inpatient treatment impractical.

Usually, detoxification centers are hospital based. There is a category considered social detoxification, where the intervention is not medically based but simply provides a safe environment for the substance-dependent individual to obtain a few days drug free. This intervention is used with substances such as cocaine that do not require a medical intervention.

Residential and Inpatient Treatment Centers

A residential treatment center is usually less medically monitored than an inpatient facility. Frequently, residential treatment is longer than inpatient. And as a general rule and because there is less psychiatric monitoring, residential does not cater to the dually diagnosed (those with a mental health diagnosis as well as a substance use disorder). Both are facilities where the client is kept 24 hours a day for anywhere from several days to months.

Inpatient may last for as little as a couple of days to several weeks. Generally, it does not last more than 28 days. Nurses are on site, often 24 hours a day. Psychiatric care is available, usually daily, and everyone receives an evaluation.

Residential treatment can also be short term, lasting only a few days or weeks to up to 18 months. Residential treatment that is long term is often a therapeutic community, which is still predominantly used in a forensic inpatient setting. A therapeutic community is based on a token economy (points or rewards are given and taken away based on behavior) and on residents being responsible for one another.

Another type of residential treatment is religious based. These facilities are often long term and use their religious morals and behaviors to help the client overcome his addiction.

Partial Hospitalization

In partial hospitalization, the client attends the therapeutic milieu of an inpatient facility (usually 6 to 8 hours per day), while leaving in the late afternoon and spending the night at home. Simply, they attend the groups and other therapy sessions that their inpatient resident compatriot is attending, but when the inpatient resident has dinner, attends the evening meetings, and sleeps at the treatment center, the partial hospitalization client goes home, to return the next day.

Intensive Outpatient (IOP)

Intensive outpatient consists of at least 9 hours of therapy weekly. Typically, therapy is 3 hours of group, three nights per week. Educational group and process group are generally conducted nightly. This has become a preferred level of care for substance use, either as a step down from inpatient or the beginning of the therapeutic experience.

Traditional Outpatient

Traditional outpatient consists of anywhere from a 1-hour session monthly to as many as 6 hours of therapy a week. It consists of either group or individual, or a combination of both (as long as it does not exceed 9 hours weekly, which would then be IOP). It is often the last stage of therapy, although one must be aware that someone might enter this level of care without being aware of the severity of the substance use issue, thus requiring a higher level. When it is the last stage of therapy, the focus is on relapse prevention, and goals and issues not seemingly directly related to substance use (such as creating a greater quality of life). When it is the initial contact with therapy, the clinician may be moving the client into the next stage of change, such as from precontemplation to contemplation, where he or she might consider a more appropriate level of care.

Assessments

Assessment is a key component in the treatment of addiction. The foremost benefit of assessment is to arrive at an accurate diagnosis of the substance use disorder. With that, the severity of the addiction invariably will determine the type of treatment necessary for the individual. It is also likely that the individual who presents with a substance use disorder can present with another mental health disorder. The presence of substance abuse disorder and another mental health disorder (e.g., depression, anxiety, PTSD) is called **comorbidity**. According to the results from the 2014 *National Survey on Drug Use and Health*, nearly 40% of individuals with substance use disorders also presented with co-occurring mental health disorders (Substance Abuse and Mental Health Services Administration [SAMSHA], 2014). Understanding the full clinical presentation of an individual is critical in determining not just the type of treatment necessary, but also establishing appropriate treatment planning to address both mental health disorders. This is essential in the process of treatment since the success of sobriety is hinged on the minimization of the co-occurring mental health issues. As such, assessments are administered throughout treatment in order to guide the treatment process and provide immediate feedback reflecting the degree of success in treatment. This approach, also known as **measurement-based care**, has proven to be the most evidence-based form of treatment that increases the likelihood of successful outcomes (Harding, Rush, Arbuckle, Trivedi, & Pincus, 2011).

Although there are innumerable assessment measures for substance abuse, the following are the most commonly used. These assessments generally have sound reliability and validity, which positions them to be the clinician's preferred choice.

Drug Use Screening Inventory (DUSI)

The Drug Use Screening Inventory (DUSI) is a 140-item dichotomous test that measures drug and alcohol use. The instrument is designed to measure severity across 10 domains: substances abuse, psychiatric disorders, behavioral problems, school adjustment, health status, work adjustment, peer relations, social competence, family adjustment, and leisure (Tarter, 1990). It is designed to be administered to those 10-years-old and up. The revised version, DUSI-R, includes the Lie Scale and contains 159 items. It takes approximately 20 minutes to complete this inventory.

Brief Addiction Monitor (BAM)

The Brief Addiction Monitor is a 17-item instrument designed to assess for risk factors, protective factors, and current use (Center of Excellence in Substance Abuse Treatment and Education, 2010). Such an assessment is ideal for utilization throughout treatment to inform the direction of intervention. First developed in the Department of Veterans Affairs (VA) system, this 5-minute monitoring tool is gaining momentum in the field as initial studies find it to possess acceptable statistical characteristics (Cacciola et al., 2013).

Addiction Severity Index (ASI)

The Addiction Severity Index (ASI) is a structured interview designed to assess severity of the substance use and other contributing life factors (McLellan, Luborsky, Woody, & O'Brien, 1980). Training is required in order to administer this 45–90-minute instrument. The ASI has shown to be valid when asking questions about the past 30 days of drug and alcohol use, as well as medical, employment, financial, psychiatric, social and family, and legal problems.

Alcohol Use Disorder Identification Task (AUDIT)

The Alcohol Use Disorder Identification Task (AUDIT) is a brief measure that boasts strong psychometric properties (Barbor, Biddle-Higgins, Saunders, & Monteiro, 2001). It was first published in 1993 as a collaborative effort among six countries as a World Health Organization project to assess for alcohol-related problems (Saunders, Aasland, Babor, de la Fuente, & Grant, 1993). There are various versions of the AUDIT, which include AUDIT-3 (3 questions), AUDIT-4 (4 questions), AUDIT-Primary Care (5 questions), AUDIT-C (10 questions), and the traditional AUDIT (10 questions). They are among the most widely used and recommended alcohol use questionnaires.

Michigan Alcoholism Screening Test (MAST)

The Michigan Alcoholism Screening Test (MAST), in its original form, is a 25-item assessment designed to detect alcoholism (Selzer, 1971). Other versions include the Brief MAST (10 items) and the Short MAST (13 items). A versatile instrument, the MAST can be used in both inpatient and outpatient settings, as well as with the geriatric population (Bommersbach, Lapid, Rummans, & Morse, 2015).

South Oaks Gambling Screen (SOGS)

The South Oaks Gambling Screen (SOGS) is the most widely used screener for gambling addiction (Lesieur & Blume, 1987). It is a 20-item self-assessment that is designed to measure pathological gambling according to the DSM-III criteria. Now in its third edition, the SOGS-3 has been translated in multiple languages and measures areas such as difficulty with family, financial difficulties, difficulty controlling spending, and deceitful behaviors. Given the significant changes between the DSM-III and the DSM-5, research is underway to extend the validity and reliability studies. Meanwhile, it still remains one of the most popular gambling screeners.

Sexual Addiction Screening Test-Revised (SAST-R)

The Sexual Addiction Screening Test (SAST) was developed in 1983 by Dr. Patrick Carnes in order to address the assessment needs of the sexual addiction population. The revised version, SAST-R, was designed to be more inclusive of sexual orientation and gender (Carnes, Green, & Carnes, 2010). The assessment was developed based on Carnes' understanding of sexual addiction, which includes fantasy, ritualization, compulsive sexual behavior, and despair (Carnes, 1983). Although reliability and validity studies for the SAST-R need to be more expansive, it still remains one of the most widely utilized measures of sex addiction.

Internet Addiction Test (IAT)

The Internet Addiction Test (IAT) was developed by Dr. Kimberly Young in 1998. As the leading pioneer in the Internet addiction field, Young was the first to present the notion of Internet addiction to the American Psychological Association. She established this assessment based on the DSM-IV criteria for substance abuse. This 20-item instrument is the most internationally used and researched Internet addiction measure. To date, there are also validation studies of the IAT for the German, Korean, Chinese, French, Turkish, Malaysian, and Portuguese populations.

Summary

There are several ways people come into addiction recovery, regardless of their motivation. Some seek formal treatment, whether **it is de**tox, inpatient rehabilitation, or outpatient counseling. Some enter outpatient counseling as a result of other issues that have been caused or exacerbated by the substance use, such as marital issues or depression. Enter recovery can be through a professional therapist or through their religious affiliation and pastoral services. Once the substance use issue is detected, they may be referred to someone with experience in helping substance users.

Some people enter recovery without formal treatment. This can be through a 12-step program like Alcoholics Anonymous or Narcotics Anonymous. Others simply stop on their own without help.

Many people who enter addiction treatment are forced into treatment by outside entities, such as the courts or even concerned family members. This is not an uncommon course of treatment. Many enter treatment externally motivated, placate their motivators, and then stop treatment, never having any desire to change. Additionally, the clinician is sometimes not effective in engaging the client in treatment. Although often clients aren't ready to be engaged, some responsibility falls on the clinician as well. Thus, it behooves the clinician to utilize assessments to help diagnose, plan treatment, and measure outcomes. In doing so, the individual will have a greater likelihood of reducing recidivism using a measurement-based care approach.

Unfortunately, the recovery process will still assume multiple relapses. It is crucial, however, to accept those relapses as part of the recovery process rather than a failure of it. This topic will be returned to later when we discuss the recovery process.

Key Terms

Substance use disorders

Substance-induced disorders

Impaired control

Social impairment

Risky use

Pharmacological criteria

Tolerance

Withdrawal

Addiction

Bottom

Low bottom

Detox

External motivation

Internal motivation

Precontemplation

Contemplation

Preparation

Action

Maintenance

Relapse (Stage Six)

Comorbidity

Measurement-based care

CHAPTER TWO

How Do People Develop an Addiction?

Learning Objectives

- Explain the concept of the disease model.
- Explain the biomedical theory.
- Understand social learning theory.
- Identify components of personality theory.
- Identify the steps to challenge thinking in addiction.
- Understand the self-medication theory.
- Explain the effect trauma has on substance use.
- Understand the psychodynamic explanation of the development of addiction.
- Explain the family systems theory.

Introduction

Embarking on the journey of understanding how people develop addiction can be much like trying different cars before you buy one. The array of theoretical explanations of addiction is vast. Whether it is understanding addiction as a disease or the result of environment, it is clear that the nature of addiction is more significant that its symptoms themselves. Professionally, the disease model is the premise for the American Psychiatric Association's diagnostic criteria found in the DSM-5. However, treatment of addiction may vary based on the type of substance or activity to which the individual is addicted.

The Disease Concept

The disease concept is a broad model that encompasses many other theoretical explanations of addiction. The concept of **disease** itself is defined as an ongoing condition that increases in severity and may result in harm or death. It is this model that first introduced the notion of abstinence to prevent relapse. The **disease model**, also known as the medical model, has been adapted by the American Psychiatric Association. Through this, the diagnostic criteria for substance use disorders were formulated. Many who attend 12-step meetings believe in the disease concept and believe they are biologically different from "normal" people. The concept of addiction as a disease has its share of controversy. Because there are no blood tests for mental illness and as substance dependence is considered a mental disorder, many deny the validity of any mental illness as a disease.

However, there is also much evidence to suggest that there are biological aspects of all mental illness, and addiction is no exception. The theory of genetic influence suggests that the root of addiction is biological. A biological trait is carried in the family genetic code, which can determine eye color, height, medical problems (diabetes, high blood pressure, etc.), and even addiction. This is also called **heredity**. Further, the more people in the family who have a substance use problem, the greater the genetic predisposition.

Some important studies have furthered the theory of genetic predisposition. These include twin studies, and studies of sons of alcoholic fathers and the processing of alcohol by their bodies, as well as early genetic coding research (Verhulst, Neale, & Kendler, 2015). In studies of nicotine use, a study indicated those with a specific genetic marker smoked more and experienced more severe nicotine withdrawal than the control group of smokers without the genetic marker.

More advanced research has implied that genetic predisposition largely influences the specific substance of choice. This explains why some people would prefer cocaine and other stimulants versus heroin or other opiates.

Biomedical Theory

The **biomedical model** combines both the biological and behavioral aspects of addiction. It purports that when an individual uses substances for a prolonged period of time, there are neurochemical and structural changes in the brain. When a chemical substance is introduced, existing neurotransmitters will either increase or diminish production. In some cases, the new substance will block the reuptake of the naturally occurring chemicals. This causes the brain to strive for a new homeostasis. In doing so, the brain resets its natural state and incorporates the substance as part of the norm. When the substance is no longer present, it elicits withdrawal symptoms that perpetuate the cycle of use.

Simply put, the person who has been using substances sets a new norm for his brain chemistry. The lack of neurotransmitter activity when the drug is absent

FIGURE 2.1. Using substances alters brain chemistry, which can create a new "normal" for the brain.

results not only in physically notable withdrawal symptoms but also mood negativity (anxiety, depression, apathy, fatigue) that make use of the substance more attractive. The addicted individual ends up using substances to feel what he now considers normal.

Having a new baseline of "normal" causes an individual to experience protracted withdrawal when the substance is not present in his or her system. **Protracted withdrawal** includes symptoms such as insomnia, depressed mood, anxious mood, irritability, or cognitive problems such as trouble concentrating. Many of these symptoms are a result of the altered neurotransmission in the brain caused by the substance use. Although these symptoms clear up with time, the amount of time may vary depending on the individual and the substance. Clients who are experiencing these symptoms are susceptible to relapse. Their brain chemistry is altered, and their mood, without substances, is not what they would consider within a normal range. The addicted individual feels different on drugs, and this contributes to increased urges or craving to use.

Social Learning Theory

The **social learning theory** proposes that addiction is a learned response that can develop from as early as childhood. It is a person's environment that vastly influences his development. For example, a child who watched his or her caretakers or other role models cope with life through the use of substances can learn to do the same. Much of what is observed is how to escape from life's difficulties. However, it is not always this simple; siblings who are exposed to the same substance-abusing caretakers do not necessarily develop substance use problems. Other factors that may influence the difference among siblings may be parent/child relational styles, school environments, intrinsic motivation, and

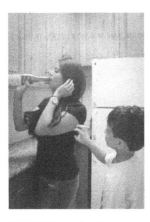

FIGURE 2.2. Another theory of addiction proposes that chemical use is learned, often from role models.

peer relations. Preadolescents and adolescents are largely susceptible to peer influence because at these ages their identity is being formed. Also, a lack of nurturing in childhood leaves an adolescent vulnerable to the influences of others.

We are a society wherein a high percentage of children consume alcohol before graduating high school, albeit a decline from the 1990s: In 2017, the number of 8th, 10th, and 12th graders who reported drinking in the 30-day period prior to the survey were 8%, 20%, and 33% respectively (Johnston et al., 2018). Alcohol isn't the only substance abused in high school. Among 12th graders, one in 17 smoke marijuana daily, and one in ten consume marijuana via vaping (Johnston et al., 2018). It is no wonder the rates of marijuana use are so high among our youth given that 65% of Americans view marijuana as morally acceptable (Jones, 2018). These statistics alone indicate that many people begin with alcohol or marijuana, which are potential gateway drugs, as teens and engage with a seeming moral freedom.

If we just look at alcohol, it is easy to see how our culture perpetuates the use of this substance. It is advertised on television. The image created is one that to truly enjoy life, one must indulge in its use. It is a sign of success (certain liquors and wines), it is a social lubricant making it easier to engage others at parties or social events, and it signifies an off-duty attitude that just makes everything more fun. Of course, this is true in some cases. But for many, it becomes the only way to cope with their otherwise painful lives. Statistically, 10% of the population of drinkers consume 50% of the alcohol sold.

Another way society contributes to the use of substances is with the idea of immediate gratification. This is evidenced by the amount of debt—especially with credit cards—our population accumulates. And this is also evidenced by "instant everything."

Additionally, our society is moving away from blindly following authority. As a result, just because people say drugs are bad, this no longer stops many from trying and possibly becoming addicted to them. In fact, there is evidence to suggest programs such as DARE, which purports a generic "drugs are bad" message, do more harm than good (Lynam et al., 1999). Demonizing marijuana has sometimes resulted in experimentation with more harmful substances. Let us explain: When kids are told how bad marijuana is and then come to know either firsthand or through a friend that using it doesn't result in the harsh consequences described in programs geared at scare tactics, the person then questions what they have been taught about other substances. Teens question authority. And when the authority has perpetrated exaggerations and embellished the truth, the teen may no longer trust anything the authority said.

This leads to the next point about American culture: the avoidance of emotional and physical discomfort. There has been a lot written in the therapeutic realm on this, and it could probably be discussed in more detail, but it seems common knowledge that people tend to avoid pain and uncomfortable feelings. Unfortunately, in this culture, it is often done to an unhealthy level. This is not to say it is not normal, but not everything that is normal is healthy. Normal just means the majority of people do it, and it is accepted socially.

So, accepting the premise that avoiding uncomfortable feelings is normal and that many teens use a substance before reaching adulthood, and additionally understanding alcohol and drugs do work in that they relieve, mask, or help the user avoid uncomfortable or painful states, it stands to reason that many people would be susceptible to the use of a substance.

Many who become addicted grew up in households where substance use was apparent, if not promoted. Even those who do not grow up in a substance-abusing household may gravitate toward a crowd of friends who used substances. As mentioned, adolescents are often susceptible to peer pressure. Most substance users experience their first use either with a family member or with a peer.

Personality Theory

Personality can be described as a set of characteristics that are pervasive and consistent throughout an individual's life. These characteristics are largely evident in a person's thoughts, behaviors, and feelings. Many theories exist regarding the origin and development of an individual's personality. Some theorists believe that each person is born with the genetic makeup of a personality type, and the life of that person is shaped by that personality style.

Frankie is a 27-year-old Italian American male who was born and raised in New York City. Frankie battled with substance abuse throughout his teen years as he experimented with and then used marijuana, alcohol, and cocaine frequently. At age 21, he "bottomed" when he totaled his car one morning at 3:00 a.m., crashing head on into a pole while going 45 miles per hour. He fractured his pelvis and broke two ribs. This resulted in his limited mobility for 6 months. The trauma of the incident was enough motivation for Frankie to realize that he will never use drugs or alcohol again. And he didn't. While working through his recovery, Frankie gained 45 pounds. He found himself turning to food for comfort. His health care providers were trying to discourage him from overeating, but he was never self-aware enough to recognize that he was becoming fat. He found that his temper was gradually becoming more out of control. His friends and family found it more and more difficult to be around him. Frankie finally turned away from overeating when the girl he was interested in told him that he wasn't her type; she preferred men who were more fit. This damaged Frankie's ego so much that he became overly motivated in physical therapy and then began working out every day. Frankie noticed that he experienced a "high" when he would push himself lifting weights. He felt that this was the best compromise he could achieve, since working out is "healthy." After many years of weightlifting, Frankie began competing on an amateur level. His diet became strict and regimented. Frankie now has only 15% body fat, works out two to three times per day, and has limited relationships. In Frankie's opinion, this is the healthiest he has ever been. However, to ask his family, they observe him as being seemingly addicted—again.

Other theorists believe that personality is shaped through the environment or external stimuli. The more popular and most widely accepted theory is the **biopsychosocial model** of personality. Simply put, the individual's personality is formed and shaped through genetic, psychological, and environmental factors. A person will have the genetic predisposition to behave and feel a certain way in response to his environment (Buckner, Heimberg, Ecker, & Vinci, 2013). A healthy personality is evident in individuals who can balance their emotions, tolerate anxiety, relate to others, function independently, and strive for growth. When considering the typical personality of addicts, one might see an imbalance or a polar expression of these factors. This is sometimes called the **addictive personality**. Characteristics often present in an addictive personality are impulsivity, high-risk behavior, narcissistic rage, emotional instability, and chronic feelings of emptiness (Kerr, 1996).

Self-Medication Theory

The **self-medication theory** maintains that people become addicted to a substance as a result of self-medicating an underlying mental health issue. Among the most common co-occurring diagnoses are bipolar disorders, depressive disorders, and anxiety disorders. These issues may or may not have been diagnosed prior to the substance use. The premise of the theory is that people will use certain substances in order to achieve a sense of relief from the psychological duress they are experiencing (Frone, 2016). This issue is salient with relapse prevention. Often, when someone is using substances for self-medication purposes, in resolving the substance use issue the psychological distress is exposed. This is typically when the person will resort to using drugs again, unless there is an intervention that teaches the individual how to cope with these psychological issues.

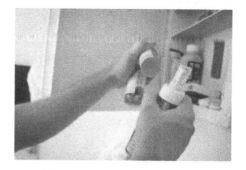

FIGURE 2.3. Self-medication theory purports substances are used to manage underlying psychological symptoms.

There is a very high correlation between addiction and other mental health issues—especially depression, anxiety, and schizophrenia, not to mention other personality disorders. Personality disorders are generally considered less debilitating than the other mental health disorders, but they are also more pervasive in that they are rigid ways of being that are often difficult to change. Some people view that generally there are two ways this occurs: the addiction came first and the resulting changes in the brain led to these other disorders, or the mental health issue preexisted the substance use, and the substance use was a coping mechanism for this other issue. Either way, the individual is now faced with dual problems. Discussion of the importance of addressing co-occurring illnesses will occur in a later chapter. For our purposes currently, you need only understand that some people begin substance use to cope with these other issues.

Frequently, young clients who have a substance abuse issue surrounding marijuana enter treatment (at the behest of their parents). Interestingly, many felt like social outcasts until trying it. Several had difficulty in social relations, had trouble initiating or sustaining conversations, and/or had fears of rejection that inhibited their socializing. One such client is Lou. Lou is a 20-year-old single Hispanic male who lives with his parents. Lou doesn't report having many friends, but reports good relationships with those he has. Lou reported moving a lot, and that because many of his classmates already knew one another, he felt like an outcast. At the age of 16, Lou was introduced to marijuana and nearly instantly had a small group of friends. He felt more at ease, laughed and joked, and although still on the quiet side, came further out of his shell.

He reports that is family is important to him and that generally he has a good relationship with them. At present, Lou's family insists on therapy, as he is using marijuana and they are very much against it. They report he is using it in their home, and they fear legal problems and believe it has a negative effect on Lou. His family reports he isn't going anywhere in his life, isn't doing well in college, and isn't working. They believe his use of marijuana inhibits his desire to look for a job and believe it will inhibit his obtaining a job due to drug screenings. Lou feels marijuana isn't a drug issue and is certainly not the root of any of his troubles.

At this time, Lou believes ceasing marijuana is not a viable option, as his friends use, he enjoys it, and he does not feel it is an issue. Lou had been experiencing social anxiety and has been self-medicating with marijuana.

Trauma

Childhood or adolescent trauma, such as sexual and/or physical abuse, death of a parent or parents, divorce, for example, may result in addiction (Banducci, Hoffman, Lejuez, & Koenen, 2014). Adult trauma, such as death of a partner or difficulty coping with changes in life like divorce or retirement, can also result in addiction. Any of these can result in lowered feelings of self-worth or the use of substances to cope with what are often unmanageable feelings.

Many clients who present for addiction treatment point to this theory as at least a contributor to their addiction. It is good practice to discuss their history with clients who enter treatment for substance use and to explore the history's relationship to the theories of addiction. In working with a varied array of clients, one will undoubtedly hear horrible stories of abuse and neglect. Clients have discussed how their parents prostituted them for money. Others have been sexually abused at the hands of their fathers, brothers, and other family members. In fact, studies have indicated that 75% of women in addiction treatment report a history of sexual abuse (Fisher & Harrison, 2009).

Clients report being beaten with switches (thin branches from a tree), extension cords, paddles, and kitchen utensils. Some have been beaten on the face and back as punishment. Examples of abuse by those entering substance use treatment are endless, but the point is made. Even those who have not endured such physical abuse have often experienced emotional and verbal abuse. Many were told by parents that they were worthless, that the parents wished they had never had them, that they are just like a hated (and often absent) parent. Again, the list could go on.

Then there are the children given up by their parents or who lose a parent to an accident. There are the broken homes, the absent fathers or mothers, and those who were shipped from family member to family member, feeling unwanted. Sometimes clients simply speak of an emotionally detached parent, one who seemed to barely notice the child was there. Of course, sometimes the now-adult child explains this away as the parent being consumed with family worries, paying the bills, or simply working a lot to make ends meet.

FIGURE 2.4. "Studies … confirm a consistent relationship between maltreatment and substance abuse." (Alvarez-Alonso et al., 2015)

An excellent example of trauma as the major contributor to a substance abuse problem is the elderly woman who had been sneaking an abusable substance into the hospital. She had been admitted as the result of a fall to a medical-surgical floor of a local hospital, which also had a substance abuse program. This 70-year-old woman had smuggled Xanax into her hospital room. Although she had informed the doctor of her prescription for it, her hospital physician had determined that she would only receive the medicine as needed, which he did not believe would be as necessary since she was in the hospital resting and shouldn't experience as much stress and anxiety. When the substance was found, the doctor ordered a substance abuse consultation with a counselor from the program.

When her substance abuse history was discussed, she reported being prescribed this substance when her husband died a couple of years earlier. She had no prior substance abuse history. A simple medication was prescribed to help her relax and sleep after the death of her husband. It came to be relied upon as a result of the trauma she experienced and the uncomfortable feelings she was living with (grief, fear). No malicious trauma, just life as it is experienced by anyone.

Many clients defend their upbringing. These clients often discuss how loving and good their parents were and how supportive they are. It is not to say this is never true. Again, parents may be all of those things and still make mistakes. The child's temperament also factors in. For example, a child who was rarely disciplined may develop problems as a result of becoming spoiled. Even a child who seems to be disciplined in the most fair and just ways can develop problems if he has a sensitive temperament. Many different factors contribute to the experience of children and their processing of the event. In parenting, there is no surefire way to assure the processing is healthy for the child. This processing, and errors in care, may later result in some unhealthy core beliefs for the child, contributing to uncomfortable feelings, which lend them susceptible, in this culture, to the abuse of substances. But again, there is no way to perfectly parent a child.

One last thought about trauma and its effect on the development of a substance use problem: All traumas are not malicious. Life can be traumatic.

Psychodynamic Explanation

Through the psychodynamic lens, substance use is a function of overwhelming and intolerable emotion. The person will turn to substances as a form of self-soothing. As that person will discover, varying effects will be experienced based on the specific substance. For example, narcotics are typically used to help manage rage or loneliness, while cocaine and other stimulants are typically used to manage depression, boredom, or emptiness. The overarching message is that emotions are unbearable for addicts. Krystal and Raskin (1970) described addicts as having a defective stimulus barrier. A person with average affective development has found a way to differentiate, desomatize, and verbalize his or her emotions. The theory of defective stimulus barrier suggests that addicts are unable to manage emotion and use substances to stave off affective flooding. This leads to the explanation as to why addicts relapse; once the person becomes physiologically clean of the substance, psychological forces resurface. As some would say, the reasons why the person began using all come back.

Another psychodynamic explanation involves looking at the addict from an object relations perspective. This perspective describes self and others; as a person develops, he finds a balance between his individuality/differentiating from others and having a healthy attachment to others. Furthermore, it describes how people view others in their external environment, as well as how they maintain the memory of significant others of the past. This lends itself to the idea that there is a world of relationships within ourselves at an unconscious level that is either congruent or incongruent with our "real" self and the external world. The ideal self is created as the fantasy of who we want to be. At times, this ideal self can incorporate aspects of an ideal object (person). Wurmser (1974) suggested that addicts experience a narcissistic crisis because of a collapse of the ideal object. Kohut (1971) purported that drugs and alcohol serve a narcissistic function to help replace the defective psychological structure. So, when a person's ideal self and internalized structure become unstable, he turns to alcohol and drugs to help give the sense of a more stable internal environment. However, once the effects of the drugs wear off, the awareness of internal instability resumes.

Mike is a 32-year-old married Cuban male. He currently works as an accountant in a large metropolitan firm. He is described by his coworkers and family as mild mannered and emotionally closed off. He is a top producer in the firm and is known to focus mostly on his work. Socially, Mike is limited. He has one person who identifies as his friend. His wife feels that she doesn't really know her husband despite being married to him for four years. Her greatest complaint is the "switch" that occurs when Mike drinks. She states that he becomes "obnoxious, conceited, and unbearable." Mike, on the other hand, enjoys drinking because he feels that's when he becomes himself.

The reality is, Mike was dominated by his parents as a child. He did not feel like he had a voice and could not express himself to his parents while growing up without adverse consequences. At the age of 19, Mike discovered that alcohol returned his strength to speak his mind. As time passed, Mike lost the majority of his friends because their experience was very similar to his wife's experience. His wife stated that the man she married is the man he is without drinking. Mike doesn't appreciate his wife's opinion because he feels that person is not his true self. When his wife asked Mike to give up drinking, Mike said, "No way. I only feel like I'm me when I drink."

In his book *The Heart of Addiction*, Lance Dodes (2002) discusses what he believes results in addiction. He describes addiction as a person's response to powerlessness in his or her life. His theory, although simply put here, discusses how childhood feelings of extreme powerlessness (often a result of abuse) are experienced again in adulthood. When individuals experience these strong feelings of powerlessness, they resort to the use of substances to exercise their power (combined with the initial stress-relieving tendencies of the substance) to do what they want. Substance use feels powerful to them. Perhaps it is the rebellion, perhaps it is just doing something they believe is completely for themselves, but whatever the reason, it feels like an exercise in demonstrating one's power.

This theory has merit, as many people experiencing addiction (not all, but many) experience childhood or adolescent abuse of some kind. This theory also has merit because using substances does relate to feelings of power. In addition to the reasons above, there is the power the substance often provides in and of itself. (Think of someone who has consumed a few drinks who is boasting and challenging others or the person on cocaine who feels invincible.)

Family Systems Theory

Although the role of family in addiction is discussed in more detail in Chapter 11, it is important to introduce it here. Family systems theory proposes that the family system, out of need, creates a situation where a scapegoat is needed. Often this occurs as a result of marital discord, but this does not always have to be the case. One of the children accepts the role of scapegoat, and because a substance use problem is one way in which attention and blame can be drawn, in some cases this is the avenue chosen.

Once the child (the word *child* here is used to represent the offspring of the parents, not necessarily to denote an age) adopts the role of scapegoat and chooses substances as that avenue, the problem develops. This draws attention from what family therapists view as the *real* problem: a severely dysfunctional family system. As long as the scapegoat creates problems, the family can focus on him (the identified patient) and not on the real issue. This is all unconscious; members are rarely aware this is occurring. Despite the focus on the identified patient and a seeming desire for him to get better, the family needs him to remain a problem. This results in somehow reinforcing the substance use problem and/or sabotaging behavior to arrest the substance use or addiction.

This theory requires that the family be treated rather than just the individual. If the individual were to receive treatment individually, the family would either unconsciously pressure the identified patient toward relapse, or if that is unsuccessful, create a new scapegoat/identified patient. As the dysfunction in the family is the problem, it is the family—and the real underlying issues— that need to be addressed. This theory and interventions are more thoroughly discussed in Chapter 11.

Summary

Although these theories help shed light on potential causes for addiction, they are not all-inclusive, nor do they explain every case. Hopefully, this chapter has shed some light on a few of the many theories that try to explain how addiction comes to be. Surely there is not one theory that adequately explains addiction for each and every person who becomes addicted. It is believed that often several of these theories combine to foster an addiction in an individual. Certainly, there are some people for whom only one of these theories is the only one that is accurate. But generally, it seems these theories often overlap, and more than one might apply to the individual.

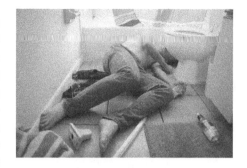

FIGURE 2.5. Addiction is a debilitating problem. In order to best help the addict, it is important to understand what he/she believes led to his/her addiction.

No one develops in a vacuum. Everyone is affected by others, and by life itself. There are several theories that view addiction as a family disease and that the substance use serves a purpose for the entire family, not just the substance user. There are other theories that address societal influence. Perhaps the child, or now teen, is susceptible to peer pressure, and thereby engages in substance use and then develops the risk for a substance abuse issue. What is essential to glean from this is the importance of looking at what influences the decisions one makes. Are people responsible for their decisions? The answer is "yes," with the following qualification: They are responsible to the degree they understand what goes into their decisions. And in that answer lies the problem and the solution: helping those with a substance use problem break through their distorted reality, understand themselves, and make insightful and educated decisions.

Key Terms

Disease	Protracted withdrawal	Biopsychosocial model
Disease model	Biomedical model	Addictive personality
Heredity	Social learning theory	Self-medication theory

CHAPTER THREE

Process Addiction

Learning Objectives

- Define process addiction.
- Understand the diagnostic nuances of process addiction in the DSM-5.
- Identify the concept of Internet addiction and its subtypes.
- Describe shopping addiction.
- Understand how sex can develop into an addiction.
- Identify the undergirding of love addiction.
- Describe the nature of exercise addiction.
- Understand the intricacies of social media addiction.

Introduction

Process addiction is described as a pattern of maladaptive behavior that results in negative consequences similar to those of substance use disorders. Examples of process addictions include gambling, surfing the Internet, shopping, sex, and exercise, to name a few. In the past, the American Psychiatric Association classified behavioral addiction as an impulse control disorder in *the Diagnostic and Statistical Manual of Mental Disorders–Fourth Edition, Text Revised* (DSM-IV-TR) and only recognized the following: intermittent explosive disorder, kleptomania, pyromania, pathological gambling, trichotillomania, and impulse-control disorder not otherwise specified (NOS) (American Psychiatric Association, 2000).

When working with clients who present with an addictive behavioral pattern, it is helpful to consider the following in order to determine whether they have an addiction:

1. Do they have an excessive preoccupation with the activity?
2. Do they experience tension, buildup, or anxiety prior to engaging in the activity?
3. Do they experience euphoria, excitement, relief, or gratification during or after engagement?
4. Have social, academic, or occupational roles been affected by this behavior?
5. Do they continue to engage in these activities despite negative consequences?
6. Are they unable to stop the behavior?

These questions are intended to be a guideline to consider whether the person suffers from a process addiction. Often, there will be co-occurring symptoms, such as depression or anxiety. Typically, with these clients there is a dual diagnosis (covered later in this book). For example: Axis I would be Impulse Control Disorder NOS and Major Depressive Disorder, Recurrent. Thorough biopsychosocial and self-report inventories can provide a clear picture of onset, severity, and duration. Knowing this will guide the course of treatment with greater ease.

In the field, there has been much debate on whether this type of behavior can be classified as an addiction. The leading objection to identifying process addiction as an addiction is that there is no ingestion of a substance, the idea being that true addiction involves an alteration of the physiological state that most likely leads to tolerance and/or withdrawal. Specifically, "tolerance, dependence and addiction are all manifestations of brain changes resulting from chronic substance abuse and involve different brain pathways than those subserving acute drug reinforcement" (Frances, Miller, & Mack, 2005, p. 3). However, the DSM-5 has reclassified many of the once-known impulse control disorders. Below you will see a reminder of the DSM-IV-TR descriptions.

Diagnosis

DSM-IV-TR

According to the *DSM-IV-TR*, "the essential feature of Impulse-Control Disorders is the failure to resist an impulse drive or temptation to perform an act that is harmful to the person or to others" (American Psychiatric Association, 2000, p. 663). Furthermore, this diagnosis cannot be accounted for by another mental health disorder. The underlying experience as a result of the behavior is the failure to resist the impulse and resulting negative consequences. The following is a brief description of DSM-IV-TR (American Psychiatric Association, 2000) impulse-control disorders:

Intermittent explosive disorder is an aggressive impulse with a sudden onset that results in either personal harm or destruction of property in a brief period of time. Most relevant to this diagnosis is the appropriateness of the behavior. The action must be considered disproportionate to the situation.

Kleptomania is the inability to refrain from stealing nonessential items. Prior to stealing, there is a heightened state of arousal, often experienced as tension, that is then replaced with a sense of euphoria. The intention behind the act cannot be that of anger or vengeance.

Pyromania is the setting of fires that result in the experience of pleasure, gratification, or relief. These occurrences happen on more than one occasion and are approached with much fascination and curiosity about fire itself. There cannot be an ulterior motive behind the fire setting.

Pathological gambling involves a continued effort to make monetary wagers despite the overarching negative consequences. Individuals experience preoccupation, tolerance, and social/occupational difficulties. The diagnostic criteria for gambling have been used as the benchmark for defining many unrecognized process addictions.

Trichotillomania is the compulsive self-removal of one's own hair. This resulting hair loss is noticeable to others. The individual experiences a buildup of tension prior to engaging in the behavior and then a sense of pleasure or relief once the hair is removed.

Impulse-control disorder not otherwise specified (NOS) is a diagnosis given to describe other patterns of behavior that involve poor impulse control but have

FIGURE 3.1. Gambling disorder is currently the only non-substance-related disorder under the DSM-5 category "Substance Related and Addictive Disorders."

not been identified in the DSM-IV-TR. This is the category that is typically used for compulsive shopping, food addiction, exercise addiction, sex addiction, and Internet addiction.

DSM-5

A new classification has emerged in the DSM-5 to capture some of the once-known impulse control disorders: disruptive, impulse-control, and conduct disorders. The hallmarks of these disorders are the difficulties people face with controlling their emotions and behaviors, which results in the violation of others' rights. Included in this new category are intermittent explosive disorder, kleptomania, and pyromania.

Trichotillomania has been reclassified under obsessive-compulsive and related disorders. This hair-pulling disorder keeps company with excoriation disorder (skin picking), and both are considered to be repetitive behaviors that are focused on the body (American Psychiatric Association, 2013, p. 235).

Pathological gambling, now called **gambling disorder**, is a non-substance-related disorder. This classification of **non-substance-related disorder** is synonymous with process addiction. It remains the only non-substance addiction recognized by the DSM-5. However, most addiction professionals can attest to the high numbers of individuals who present with other known process addictions. In order to be considered a "disorder" in the DSM-5, a particular syndrome must have established research to support the condition. As mentioned before, many of the other process addictions are still being researched. Although, there is hope on the horizon for Internet gaming disorder; it is included in the DSM-5 as a "condition for further study."

Internet Addiction

This is a highly controversial topic. Many scholars disagree with the notion of pathological Internet use. Much of this premise is the pervasive and necessary function of the Internet in our daily lives. Traditionally, a non-substance addiction is measured by the increasing amount of engagement in the activity. Yet, with online companies, jobs, and projects, how can one escape the Internet? We communicate online, we shop online, we do research online. So, how is using the Internet for many hours a day considered an addiction?

There is an increase in case studies over the years indicating a significant issue. Kimberly Young was the first psychologist to introduce the concept of Internet addiction to the American Psychological Association with her presentation on "Pathological Internet Use: The Emergence of a New Clinical Disorder" (Young, 1996, 2015). She contended that the individuals in her research exhibited pathological behaviors when their Internet use interfered with their academic, social, financial, and occupational lives (**Internet addiction**). Further, she was able to identify particular behavioral patterns that would categorically result in negative consequences—specifically, cyber affairs. Young's research revealed underlying reasons behind the pathological behaviors, such as social support, sexual fulfilment, and creating a new persona (Young, 1997; 2015).

FIGURE 3.2. Technology Addiction is controversial, given our culture's dependency on it. Yet, studies indicate that Information Technology Addiction has 3 common factors: Withdrawal, tolerance, and impaired functioning.

Dr. Young is a notable pioneer in the field of Internet addiction and still continues to do valuable work in this area. However, other researchers soon followed after her. Griffiths (2000) considered Internet addiction to be a real phenomenon, as he observed there is a development of tolerance, the inability to decrease use despite negative consequence, and damage to social/occupational responsibilities. Davis (2001) also agreed that there is such a thing as pathological Internet use. His research yielded two major categories: specific pathological Internet use or generalized pathological Internet use. Specific use describes those individuals who have become fixed on a particular online activity, whereas general use is as it describes. Hall and Parsons (2001) also agreed that there is a pattern of dependence that can occur but felt that it was essential to conceptualize the individual from a holistic perspective.

As therapists, it is necessary to listen to the client and evaluate him with an open mind. It is helpful to utilize self-report inventories when doing so to provide support for a diagnosis in an area that is currently not uniform. An example of this is the Online Usage Inventory (OUI), which was developed using the DSM-IV-TR as a guidepost (Ramnath, 2004). This inventory (see Appendix A) was developed in order to capture a spectrum of online behavior from healthy online use to online dependence disorder. Healthy online use (HOU) is a term that describes the functional Internet behavior, cognitive flexibility, and emotional stability that does not interfere with daily living. Conversely, online dependence disorder (ODD) describes a set of addiction symptomatology observed through maladaptive cognitions, emotions, and behaviors that resulted from an individual's Internet use (Ramnath, 2004). Also measured in the OUI are subtypes:

Online Communication (OC)

This category describes users who spend the majority of their time online emailing, instant messaging, or entering chat rooms. The usage does not distinguish between the nature of the online communication—platonic, romantic, or work related.

Online Sexual Gratification (OSG)

This category refers to users who spend the majority of their online time accessing or downloading pornography, viewing or participating in virtual sex websites, or engaging in any other sexually related web activity. Any individual who may interact/communicate with another for purposes of sexual gratification (i.e., virtual sex) will also be classified in this category, not online communication.

Online Spending (OS)

This category refers to individuals who spend the majority of their time online making purchases. These purchases are to include stock trading, gambling, bidding on auctions, and music downloading, as well as buying products. An individual who excessively buys pornographic materials would still be classified in online sexual gratification, since that is the purpose of their online spending. In addition, an individual who spends money gambling online, but only against the computer, will be categorized in online spending.

Interactive Gaming (IG)

This category refers to spending most online time playing interactive computer games. This excludes games played against the computer. The games must involve at least one other individual. In addition to standard interactive games, the games may include fantasy football, poker, and blackjack. Although there may be online spending involved with some games, these individuals will still be categorized as IG as long as there is interaction with other individuals.

Information Searching (IS)

This includes those who spend the majority of their time online seeking information. The type of information they seek may include job searches, product searches, entertainment searches, news searches, sports searches, academic searches, and maps, to name a few.

Nonspecific

This includes users who do not spend the majority of their time online doing one specific activity. Rather, their time is divided equally among multiple activities.

> Maria is an 18-year-old Caucasian female who is described by most as very outgoing and affable. Within the past six months, Maria's friends have noticed that she has not hung out with them as much, nor has she even called them to just talk. Moreover, her parents have noticed that she does not join them for dinner anymore, and she avoids contact with her little brother because he always asks to use her computer. Much of Maria's time is taken up in chat rooms. She told her best friend three months ago that she feels it is much safer to talk with people on the Internet than in person. When Maria is forced to go to class by her parents, she is preoccupied with what she will talk about in the chat room later that day. As the class continues, she begins to get anxious because she has a gut feeling that she is missing out on an incredible conversation. Her grades have slipped from As to Cs. Maria's parents are concerned because they feel that they are "losing" their daughter. This is a prime example of an online dependence disorder, online communication subtype.

Identifying the degree of pathology is necessary when developing a treatment plan. Moreover, knowing what specific activity the person is engaging in can then guide the path to recovery.

Interestingly, the DSM-5 is only considering classifying **Internet gaming** as a disorder in the future. It is proposed to reflect "persistent and recurrent use of the Internet to engage in games, often with other players, leading to clinically significant impairment or distress" (American Psychological Association 2013, p. 795). As practitioners, it is imperative to consider other aspects of online use as holding the same addictive allure as do games. Simply because gaming is potentially being recognized by the DSM in the future does not mean that the other online activities are any less problematic to the individual.

Shopping Addiction

Shopping addiction, or compulsive buying, is another condition that is not recognized by the DSM-5. Nonetheless, it is an area that has been significantly researched over many years. Although there are varying criteria for what constitutes shopping addiction, the following is a set of diagnostic criteria that have been more commonly accepted (McElroy, Keck, Pope, Smith, & Strakowski, 1994):

1. A maladaptive preoccupation with buying unnecessary items or items that are not affordable, or shopping for longer periods of time to achieve the same desired effect.
2. The preoccupation or buying leads to distress or impairment.
3. The buying does not occur as a result of a manic or hypomanic episode.

It is important to consider what can be the trigger for a compulsive buyer. No longer is it simply going to a store. Now, television commercials, specific name brands, online bargains, and coupons dominate society. These triggers have become salient for those who are struggling with shopping addiction. Frequently, dissatisfaction in other areas of one's life can lead to a person turning to shopping. The euphoria experienced as a result helps to alleviate the distress that was previously experienced.

It is very common for shopping addicts to develop financial difficulties. This can lead to relationship difficulties because deceit typically accompanies the compulsive behavior. Partners will discover the behavior after a series of credit card statements or collection notices arrive to the home. Even if the individual is single, they will turn to family and friends for support. The unfortunate result is the addict feeling guilt, shame, and remorse. Bankruptcy is a common occurrence for shopping addicts.

Treatment involves identifying co-occurring disorders, which are typically mood disorders, anxiety disorders, impulse control disorders, and substance use. Once co-occurring disorders are identified, it is necessary to provide treatment for both in order to reduce the symptomatology. Treatment must have not only an insight-oriented component, but a behavioral component is necessary as well. Financial support and education are crucial for this population in order for them to recover and become more fully functioning.

Sex Addiction

Sex addiction is not recognized by the DSM-5. This, however, does not reflect the prevalence of the disorder. According to the National Association of Sexual Addiction and Compulsivity, approximately 3% to 6% of the population suffer from some form of sex addiction. According to Hook, Hook, and Hines (2008), the following criteria best describe someone who experiences sex addiction:

1. The individual experiences persistent, intense sexually arousing fantasies, urges, or behaviors.

2. The sexual fantasies, urges, or behaviors cause clinically significant distress or impairment in at least one important area of functioning.
3. Symptoms are present for at least a six-month duration.
4. The condition is not due to another medical condition or better explained by another disorder.

Eddy is a 32-year-old African American male who knows he has a vice. He loves to download pornography. He has switched jobs three times because he asked for too many advances on his paycheck. He has maxed out all of his credit cards. Yet, he still loves his porn. He is thinking about selling his baseball collection so that he can buy a faster computer that holds more memory. Eddy doesn't care that he stopped talking with the girl he's dating. He is actually relieved because he can't afford to buy her dinner, having spent all his money on downloading porn. Besides, Eddy says he much prefers chatting with women in those X-rated sex chat rooms; at least they are FREE. Three months later, after Eddy got fired from his job, he realized that he has a problem. Eddy joined a support group for sex addicts. Initially, he was hyperaroused by the women in the group because of their high sex drive. However, after he heard their pain and suffering, he quickly realized that they have issues, too. Eddy has decided to stay with the group and, hopefully, turn his life around.

When trying to understand this population, many people get hung up on the stereotypes of compulsive sexual behavior: women are perceived as "easy" and men are perceived as "studs" when engaging in excessive sexual behavior. However, for the individual, there is much greater distress that supersedes the stereotypical stigma. The need to engage in sexual activity becomes a pervasive preoccupation until satisfied. A person can engage in high-risk sexual activity (unknown partners, unprotected sex) in order to achieve alleviation from the distress. Subsequent to engaging in the activity, the person may experience shame, guilt, and remorse. Not only does this emotional experience result from his or her current behavior, but it also taps into the person's past. A significant number of individuals who suffer from sex addiction experienced sexual, physical, or emotional abuse during childhood (Bergner, 2002). An industry-standard sex addiction instrument is the Sexual Addiction Screening Test-Revised (SAST-R) developed by Patrick Carnes. This instrument was developed to help clinicians determine whether or not the sexual behavior is compulsive and if it requires treatment.

Treatment is varied when it comes to sex addiction. Modalities can range from individual psychotherapy, couples psychotherapy, family psychotherapy, group psychotherapy, or a 12-step support group. The more successful modality will depend on the specific needs of the client. What has uniformly shown to be effective is 12-step support when used as an adjunct to some form of psychotherapy. Because the area of sex addiction still carries a taboo stigma, family psychotherapy is the least popular. Most popular are individual and group psychotherapies.

Typically, group members achieve therapeutic gain from the experience of sharing their stories and hearing from others with similar struggles. Long-term group treatment has shown to have positive gains with the members. Having a long-term, platonic relationship with individuals is something that the members can bring to their everyday lives. Individual psychotherapy is beneficial to work through any childhood abuse that may be the underpinnings of the current behavior. Individual psychotherapy can also be of benefit with co-occurring disorders, such as the more common anxiety and eating disorders (Briken, Habermann, Berner, & Hill, 2007).

Love Addiction

As with most of the behavioral addictions listed here, the DSM-5 does not recognize **love addiction**. However, the 12-step support group Sex and Love Addicts Anonymous was founded in 1976. It was the first 12-step support group to directly address love addiction. Since then, a group called simply Love Addicts Anonymous has been created.

Many prominent writers in the field of addiction and relationships have questioned whether most of what this culture calls love isn't more of an addiction than actual healthy love (Peele, 1985). But for some, their behavior and internal experience related to romantic relationships becomes what they would consider an addiction.

Redcay and Simonetti (2018) differentiate between "mature love," "being in love," and "love addiction." They define mature love as attachment and companionship (similar to what Sternberg identifies as "companionate love," which will be discussed in Chapter 10). The authors concede the addictive potential of falling in love, but discriminate between what is healthy and what is addictive (Redcay & Simonetti, 2018). Although the differences are often harder to ascertain in relationships than they are in writing, these differentiations are a good place to start.

For the love addict, the infatuation at the beginning of a relationship becomes a drug. Often this individual has a stream of short-lived relations, ending the relationship when the feeling dissipates. Some remain in a committed relationship but carry out their addiction in affairs, which often provide the passion their long-term relationship lacks. Love addiction can take many forms, but the end result is the same: an obsessive and compulsive association with romantic relationships. Some indicators of a love addiction are as follows:

1. An unhealthy attachment to the passion and enthrallment of the beginning of a relationship
2. A long history of short romantic relationships; ending the relationship when or shortly after the excitement dwindles
3. Inability to stop seeing someone despite it being destructive
4. The need for a relationship to make life bearable
5. Desperation when not in a relationship
6. A feeling life has no meaning without a relationship

An issue that complicates determining if a love addiction exists is codependency. **Codependency** is defined as excessive psychological or emotional dependence on another. This term originated in reference to the partners of alcoholics but has been used for anyone who seems to depend on others for their own emotional and psychological well-being. A separate 12-step support group exists for those believing they have this malady: Codependents Anonymous. For codependency, the relationship can be with anyone: a partner, parent, sibling, one's grown child, or friend.

The difference between codependence in a partnered relationship and love addiction are that one is an addiction to love generally, and the other only occurs between two people. It is your authors' contention that since both can occur in the context of romantic relationships, either support group might help, if that is the case.

Exercise Addiction

Exercise addiction is not recognized by the DSM-5. It is, however, a maladaptive pattern of behavior that results in negative consequences. Given that exercise is recommended by most health care providers, it is easy for addicts to mask their pathology. Most people might not even realize that exercise addiction even exists. The signs, nonetheless, are as follows:

1. There is a preoccupation with exercising on a daily basis (sometimes multiple times a day).
2. Exercise is more important than other activities.
3. The person is unwilling to stop exercising despite negative consequences, such as the need to rest, injuries, or illness.

4. The amount and intensity of the exercise will increase in order to achieve a euphoric effect.
5. If the person does not exercise, he will experience withdrawal: irritability, restlessness, tension, anxiety, and sleeplessness.

Mikey is a 22-year-old Italian American male. When Mikey was 13, he was ridiculed in his school for being overweight. This teasing continued throughout his high school years. Mikey was so socially destroyed that he decided not to go to college in order to avoid the same kind of pain. After graduating from high school, Mikey began working at a yogurt store located in a strip mall. One day at lunch, Mikey took a stroll through the strip mall. He discovered a small gym. This intrigued him, and he walked in. The person at the desk encouraged him to try the gym, no risk, and let her know if he was interested after the first week. Mikey took her up on this. After one week of exercising daily, Mikey was down four pounds. At the end of the week, he became a member of the gym. Mikey continued working out there every day. The pounds were melting off of him. Five months later, Mikey had incredible muscle definition and felt incredible about himself. However, he wanted to keep going. He wanted more. Mikey began working out morning and night, every day. His muscles were fatigued and his family relationships were getting strained, yet he did not seem to mind. He felt the positive outweighed the negative. Mikey eventually developed such a maladaptive behavior pattern that he got a job at the gym, he works out multiple times throughout the day, experiences headaches and irritability if he doesn't exercise, and continues to work out despite a pulled hamstring.

Scholars postulate that it is the euphoric effect of exercising that prevents the person from stopping. The euphoria is achieved when endorphins are released. Endorphins activate opiate receptors in the brain, resulting in feelings of pain relief and ecstasy. Similar to the ingestion of a substance, the exercise addict needs to increase the amount and intensity of the exercise as time goes on to achieve the same desired effect (tolerance). Ironically, because of the physiological experience of a "high," exercise addiction is the process addiction that is most comparable to substance use disorders.

People who suffer from low self-esteem, poor body image, and eating disorders are most likely to develop exercise addiction. In addition, those who have the propensity for obsessive-compulsive behavior are just as likely to develop this addiction. Therefore, treatment of this disorder needs to be catered toward overlapping symptomatology. Providing an assessment such as the Exercise Addiction Inventory will facilitate that process (Terry, Szabo, & Griffiths, 2004).

The inventory is a six-item self-report measure that reflects attitudes and beliefs about exercise behavior. Once it is determined that a person has exercise addiction, treatment should involve behavioral modification, cognitive restructuring, and motivational interviewing.

FIGURE 3.3. Exercise addiction is often considered a "healthy addiction." However, as with other addictions, the detriment to one's life is the determining factor and is not healthy.

Social Media Addiction

Online use has become a daily function for most. In 2018, nine out of 10 Americans were online for various reasons (Hawi, Samaha, & Griffiths, 2018). One of the more popular functions online is utilizing social media. Social media is an online modality that allows users to share opinions, information, pictures, and videos. The most popular networks are Facebook, YouTube, Twitter, Instagram, LinkedIn, and Snapchat. The ways in which social media can be accessed is through either a PC, tablet, or smartphone. As discussed previously, those who exhibit pathologic use online may have Internet addiction. However, the type of Internet addiction may be specific, such as online shopping, online gaming, information searching, online gambling, online sexual gratification, and now social media. Internet gaming is proposed to be included in the next iteration of the DSM. However, a strong competitor may be **social media addiction**.

As was Internet addiction in its taxonomy youth, social media addiction also has alternative names, such as social networking addiction and problematic social media use. All names address the same issue.

According to Pew Research Center, Facebook and YouTube were the most popular social networking sites of 2018. Approximately two thirds of American adults report using Facebook, of which three quarters utilize it daily (Smith & Anderson, 2018). Although the Facebook use statistics are significant, a striking data point is that 94% of users age 18–24 use YouTube. Moreover, 88% of users age 18–29 utilize any form of social media. Given these numbers, concern for overuse is natural. When asked, 40% of users say they would find it difficult to give up social media (2018). In addition, the ease of access to social media compounds the difficulty. Before the advent of "there's an app for that," individuals needed to wait to access the Internet on their PC or tablet. Currently, there are over five billion mobile phone users internationally, over three billion are social media users, and nine out of 10 access social media via their mobile device (Kemp, 2018). When considering substance addiction, access to the substance is a significant factor. In the 1990s, the use of the Internet was becoming ubiquitous across homes and work sites. In the early 2000s, cases of Internet addiction were popping up around the world. Factor in this ballooning of social media use and ease of access, and a recipe for addiction is made.

The field is still young with respect to establishing psychometrically sound assessments for social media addiction. In 2012, the Bergen Facebook Addiction Scale (BFAS) was developed to measure social media addiction specific to Facebook. It is a 6-item questionnaire with items reflecting DSM addiction criteria (salience, mood modification, tolerance, withdrawal, and relapse) (Salem, Almenaye, & Andreassen, 2016). So far, this instrument has shown to have "adequate" psychometric properties (da Veiga et al., 2018). An offshoot of the BFAS is the Bergen Social Media Addiction Scale (BSMAS). This instrument is a more generic version of the BFAS and is designed to measure social media addiction across any of the platforms with a 6-item scale similar to the BFAS. So far, research measuring its psychometric properties are specific to different countries (i.e., Persia, Italy, Thailand). The preliminary results suggest the instrument is sufficient to measure social media addiction and appropriate for future research (Lin, Broström, Nilsen, Griffiths, & Pakpour, 2017).

Empirically validated treatment options of social media addiction are not yet available. However, studies have shown a co-occurrence of depression with pathological social media use (Shensa et al., 2017). As with established substance abuse treatments, addressing the co-occurring disorder increases the likelihood of treatment success. Personality characteristics and circumstances of those who overuse social media, such as shyness and loneliness, are beginning to be identified (Bian & Leung, 2015). The treatment implications are becoming clearer as research continues to stream in.

Summary

Process addiction is a newly explored branch in the field of addiction. Many of what would classify as process or behavior addictions have not yet been recognized by the DSM-5. The DSM-5 recognizes gambling disorder, as well as other disorders with obsessive-compulsive and impulse control problem behaviors, such as intermittent explosive disorder, kleptomania, pyromania, and trichotillomania. Yet, when it comes to Internet, shopping, sex, and exercise addictions, there are no recognized diagnoses or empirically validated treatments. In order to effectively treat people who present with these issues, it is recommended that practitioners research published studies and use self-report inventories to support their diagnosis. The challenge clinicians face is the nature of these addictions. Using the Internet, shopping, sex, and exercise are activities of daily life. Most individuals engage in one or more of these activities on a daily basis. However, when a person transcends the norm and enters into pathological behavior, the challenge becomes teaching the person how to reengage in a healthy manner. Abstinence from these activities is not a realistic option.

Key Terms

Process addiction

Intermittent explosive disorder

Kleptomania

Pyromania

Trichotillomania

Impulse control disorder NOS

Pathological gambling

Gambling disorder

Non-substance-related disorder

Internet addiction

Internet gaming

Shopping addiction

Sex addiction

Love addiction

Codependency

Exercise addiction

Social media addiction

CHAPTER FOUR

The Cognitive Processes Involved in Addiction

Learning Objectives

- Explain the effects of substance use disorders on cognitions.
- Differentiate cognitive distortions commonly found in addiction.
- Identify how cognitive distortions contribute to relapse.
- Identify the process in the "chain of behavior."
- Identify the steps to challenge thinking in addiction.
- Describe the role of mindfulness in substance use recovery.
- Use cognitive theory to conceptualize substance use disorder cases.

Introduction

Assuming that the newly recovering person has identified some of the contributors to his addiction, he is ready for the next step. Like other mental health diagnoses, pathological substance use impacts thinking. This is most obvious when the addict is using. Everyone around him may realize he has a problem, yet he denies it to others and often—most importantly—to himself. Often, the addict is the last in his circle to realize he has a problem with substances. This is the defense mechanism of **denial**. Denial is a normal defense mechanism all humans use. It is used predominantly when the reality of a situation is too overwhelming for the psyche to handle. Most people can relate to saying "no" and to believing there must be some mistake when they lose a loved one. Normally, as the psyche becomes capable of handling the reality of the situation, the defense mechanism dissolves. However, with addiction, often the defense mechanism of denial is overused and supported by other defense mechanisms.

If an addict can accept he or she has an addiction, the next step is to understand how the addiction affects his or her thinking. This is certainly true when he or she was using, but what most people have difficulty accepting is that this distorted thinking continues into early recovery and often returns even in late recovery in times of stress.

Understanding Cognition

A noteworthy book on how addicts typically think was written by Abraham Twerski and is titled, *Addictive Thinking: Understanding Self-Deception* (1997). Twerski is a renowned psychiatrist, chemical dependence counselor, rabbi, and founder of the Gateway Rehabilitation Center in Pennsylvania. His articulate description of self-deceptive thinking provides insight into the struggles of sobriety for those experiencing addiction. Here are some of the **cognitive distortions** that Dr. Twerski identifies, along with a few the authors have as well:

Hypersensitivity: A greater sensitivity to stress and a more acute feeling of emotional discomfort than those not addicted. Dr. Twerski describes it as "a sunburn of the emotions." The recovering person reacts more extremely to perceived slights and harm.

Personalizing: This is when an individual makes a neutral event seem personal, as if the event took place out of malice, without objective evidence of this having occurred. This is a common distortion of those with depression. A good example is when someone doesn't say hello to you despite your greeting them. Someone personalizing would assume the person ignored them. In truth, there may be many explanations for this, including him not hearing you or being otherwise deeply engaged in thought.

False Sense of Entitlement: This is when there is a feeling that something is owed, despite not being warranted. When someone is using, a common example is, "After a day like today, I deserve a drink." This distortion of thinking is dangerous in early recovery, as someone new to recovery may experience extreme stress. When this stress is overwhelming, they may begin to feel they deserve a break from it all and will be at a high risk for relapse.

Fortune-Telling: This distortion results in believing you know what will happen days, weeks, or months in advance. It is usually associated with a particular event combined with negative expectations, giving the addict a rationalization to use. For example, "I'm only twenty-five and can't stay clean the rest of my life, so why stay clean now?"

Projection: This is another defense mechanism, originally identified by Freud, that has particular relevance to the addicted/recovering individual. Projection occurs when someone takes characteristics particular to them and projects them onto another. An example is when an addict believes everyone is addicted to something. Another example is when someone is generally dishonest and then doesn't trust others because they believe everyone is dishonest. There have been times we have worked with addicts just entering treatment. They often ask if the therapist had a drug problem. Often, if the therapist discloses that they did, the client would question how long. The client often then quizzes the therapist about different substances: "No mar-

FIGURE 4.1. Research has found an increase in alcohol consumption when the price of alcohol is reduced during happy hour (Baldwin, Stogner, & Miller, 2014).

ijuana in ten years?" "You haven't even had a beer in ten years?" Frequently, they just said outright they didn't believe the therapist. Because they are unable to imagine this for themselves, they don't believe anyone is capable of sustained abstinence.

Catastrophizing: This distortion is another that is common to both addicts and people with depression. Catastrophizing occurs when someone takes a problem and focuses on the worst-case scenario possible, making the problem seem overwhelming and larger than it is. For example, someone might focus on her time recommended in inpatient treatment and feel she can't do that long because the family would fall apart without her, she will lose her job, the children will become homeless, and so forth. This defense mechanism is often used to provide excuses for substance use. In early recovery, catastrophizing is frequently used to rationalize and justify poor decision-making. It is also used to create drama for the recovering individual, which they have become more than accustomed to during the addiction.

Fear of Emotion: Many addicts work diligently to control their emotions, usually due to fear of becoming "out of control" with anger or sorrow. This usually leads to a repression of feelings, which can then result in a general feeling of depression.

Minimizing: This distortion entails reducing the severity of the problem or the consequences of the problem. For example, being hospitalized for a medical problem related to alcohol but focusing on the doctors making money instead as the reason one is there. I once had a client whose wife was a doctor. After he was hospitalized for pancreatitis and entered addiction treatment, he claimed the length of his stay was a result of his wife being a doctor, not the severity of his drinking problem.

Rationalization: This distortion consists of providing good reasons instead of the true reasons. This is usually presented in a believable way, and the addict often truly believes the rationalization. It is common for a client to say that he had to smoke pot or his rage would become out of control and he might seriously injure someone. You can see how this might put a new therapist at a loss for a course of action.

Justifying: This distortion occurs when explaining past or recent drug and/or alcohol use in a manner that makes it a normal reaction. The addict feels justified in the decision to use. There once was a member who introduced himself to the group and explained why he relapsed after a time in recovery. He discussed the deaths of three people close to him in a six-month period. By the time he was done, no one in the group felt they could challenge him. This was because he justified the decision to use so well that all of his peers in the group thought they might do the same thing in similar circumstances. Now, you might think this is reasonable. But that is the purpose of a good justification.

These cognitive distortions affect the way in which someone with a substance use disorder views reality. Throughout the rest of this chapter, and the book, an approach to recognizing the above distortions as well as other aspects of questioning and challenging thinking and altering perception is explored.

This approach to addiction recovery is a many-tiered approach. The first tier is a cognitive approach. The other tiers will be addressed later in the book. First, it is important to define *cognitive*. **Cognitive** simply means thoughts or thinking processes. Cognitive therapy focuses on the way in which thoughts, especially automatic thoughts, affect the way we feel and behave. The theory behind cognitive therapy is that our thoughts or perceptions about an event— often referred to as the activating event—lead to our feelings about that event. Our feelings about the event contribute to our behavior as a response to the event. Cognitive therapy seeks to teach us how to first, identify; second, challenge; and third, replace dysfunctional (unhealthy, detrimental) thoughts that lead to negative feelings and potentially detrimental behavior.

To really grasp the concept of cognition, it is necessary to be familiar with the inception of its theory. Cognitive therapy's (**CT**) founder is Aaron Beck.

While practicing therapy with depressed clients, Beck became interested in what he describes as the "automatic thoughts" of his clients. He found that these automatic thoughts were usually negative and self-deprecating in nature. Beck believed that these thoughts occurred even when they ran contrary to evidence in that situation. He came to the theory that to change dysfunctional emotions, it was best to learn to identify and directly challenge the automatic thoughts that lead to the emotions. He then identified some common cognitive distortions in depression that lead to dysfunctional emotions and behavior. After years of research, many successful cognitive therapy interventions for depressed clients were also found useful for other disorders. This prompted continued research into cognitive behavioral therapy (**CBT**) and resulted in it being the most evidence-based form of treatment across the board due to its strong empirical base (Dobson & Dobson, 2017).

With its ever-growing treatment success, cognitive behavioral therapy has gained momentum in addiction treatment. The Substance Abuse and Mental Health Services Administration (SAMHSA) recognized CBT and related practices as evidence based, and as a result, CBT is the most ubiquitous treatment approach taught to mental health practitioners (Iarussi, Tyler, Crawford, & Crawford, 2016). Because of its popularity, there are many variants of cognitive therapy (which challenge thoughts to change dysfunctional behavior) that boast success with addiction.

In the beginning of their recovery, most addicts report persistent craving. The National Institute of Drug Abuse (NIDA) has identified Terence Gorski as a leader in the field of addiction with his notable authorships and widely respected relapse prevention model. Gorski describes the following factors that contribute to addictive preoccupation that perpetuates cravings:

Euphoric recall: focusing on and exaggerating the good memories of use; also called rosy recollection

Positive expectancy: the belief that substance use will bring us pain-free pleasure, due to experiences in the early part of addiction

Trigger event: anything that causes sudden stress, pain, or discomfort

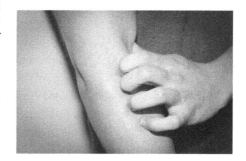

FIGURE 4.2. Itching is a common symptom of opioid withdraw.

Obsession: inability to stop thinking about using; usually fostered by euphoric recall and positive expectancy

Compulsion: a feeling process that occurs in the gut; strong, irrational desire to do something that is not in the person's best interest

Craving: a body or tissue hunger for substances

If we focus on the first two, you might be able to see how cognitive challenging might be helpful to the addict in remaining abstinent. Let's look at an example:

Perhaps a client is in early recovery. He is feeling stressed, as things are mounting up. It would be normal at this point to have a thought of substance use. So the thought creeps in. "Man, it would be great to have a drink [bowl, hit, shot, bump, etc.]." Then the substance user starts thinking how good it used to be in the past. He thinks of all the good times, the relief, the laughing, the euphoria, and the high. *This is euphoric recall.* Then the client starts to think how if he had some (alcohol, pot, coke, Xanax, heroin, blues), it would be great. He would get high, everything would melt away temporarily, and he would get some relief from all this stress. *This is positive expectancy.* And this is distorted thinking.

The following is related to the distortions of euphoric recall and positive expectancy:

Jenny, a 35-year-old Caucasian female, drank in college and for a number of years after. And up until five years ago, she still enjoyed drinking. It meant time with family and friends, relief from daily stress, enjoyable interactions, and pleasurable experiences. But for the last five years, Jenny had struggled with suicidal ideation, drunken rages at others, the threat of a lost career, and embarrassing behaviors. She had been in and out of recovery. She was feeling like a "chronic relapser." (As an aside, whenever we hear a client say she or he is a chronic relapser, we immediately make them change the verbiage to "I used to be a chronic relapser.")

When Jenny discussed her thoughts prior to a relapse, she would describe sitting in front of the liquor store and remembering the great times she had, five years prior! She didn't think of the pain of the last 20 or more drinking episodes. She remembered the good times and expected that if she drank she would feel good. This was completely contrary to the evidence of the last five years. As such, it is distorted thinking. More so, Jenny expected that her experience would be as euphoric as the early days. After working to identify her cognitive distortions, she was able to see that she was experiencing euphoric recall and positive expectancy.

Think for a moment of how this client ended up seeking help for this substance issue. Yes, substances worked for a while. Yes, at times they were still effective at helping the substance-dependent person escape the pain of life or make life more exciting. But the person sought help because things had gotten out of control. When the individual is able to alter his thinking as we have done above, he is becoming more adept at cognitive challenging.

The Chain of Behavior

Rational emotive behavioral therapy (REBT) was developed by Albert Ellis in 1955. Ellis believed that cognition, emotion, and behavior were not separate processes but rather interdependent ones (Dobson, 2010). This is one of the most widely used theories when what we are concerned with is changing behavior. Initially, we want to change the behavior of accruing consequences because of drinking or using drugs. In other words, we want to become free of the consequences of the dysfunctional behavior of substance use. We learned that we have an addiction, and the only way to stop experiencing consequences resulting from drug and alcohol use is by complete abstinence from these substances. So, the behavioral concern now is to stop using substances or to keep from relapsing into their use.

Behavior is the final link in the chain. Behavior is the end result in a series of events both internal and external, which begin with our beliefs—especially core beliefs. Core beliefs refer to long standing beliefs one accepts about reality. These beliefs begin in childhood and are a result of socialization and parenting, as well as personal experiences. The diagram below illustrates the series of internal and external events, or the chain to behavior.

Activating Event
▼
Core beliefs
exist prior to event
▼
Thoughts
about the event
▼
Feelings
about the event
▼
Behavior
in reaction to the event

As can be seen by the diagram, the activating event triggers thought reactions from our core beliefs. (A leads to B in the diagram). An **activating event** can be any event that precedes thoughts and feelings. Let's say someone new to recovery is attending an educational group. If the therapist reports that he believes some of his group members are headed for a relapse, this would be an activating event. This is an activating event because it triggers thoughts in the group member. These thoughts might be "the therapist thinks I am headed for a relapse" or "I must not be working hard enough." These thoughts are flavored by one's core beliefs about oneself and others.

The same words create different reactions in different people. What is both ironic and interesting is that often when one thinks the therapist might be talking about him or her and is concerned, that person is usually doing okay. It is usually the individual who thinks "Oh, he isn't talking about me, he's talking about Joe" who is at the higher risk. The significant aspect in this is that the same words created two different reactions in these individuals partly as a result of their core beliefs.

These thoughts create feelings, and the feelings lead to the behavior (B leads to C in the diagram). This is true whether the behavior is desired or not. However, when the behavior is a desired one, we do not need to change it. For example, if we are complimented by another on a task we completed, we may focus our thoughts on positive self-statements, such as "I did a good job" or I gave it my best." These self-statements will lead to positive feelings about ourselves. Cognitive therapy focuses on identifying dysfunctional thoughts, which Beck calls cognitive distortions, as the point of attack in the chain to changing undesirable behavior (D in the diagram, which is three steps, as you will see).

Addictive thinking is not cured by the cessation of drug use. It often persists well into recovery. As these thoughts are identified and challenged (usually after techniques learned in counseling and 12-step meetings), their power over behavior diminishes. In a healthy recovery, these thoughts become little more than fleeting thoughts, which are identified and then dismissed as irrational absurdities.

Challenging cognitive distortions consists of several steps (as shown in the diagram below). The first step is identifying that it is possible you are entertaining a cognitive distortion. This is called **Detect** in the diagram for simplicity. The second step is to seek evidence that both supports and disputes your thinking. This is referred to as **Debate** in the diagram. It is imperative to look at the evidence that supports or refutes the thoughts in an objective and rational fashion. If the client is unable to look at the evidence objectively, it may be suitable for them to ask a sponsor, counselor, or peer for assistance. If the evidence found is insufficient to support the thoughts and beliefs that are entertained, the next step is to replace the dysfunctional thought with a more rational one. This is identified in the diagram as **Discriminate**.

A → B → C

Activating event   Beliefs about the event   Emotional/behavioral consequences

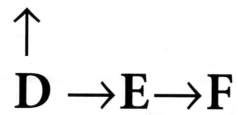

D → E → F

Disputing intervention   Effective philosophy   New feelings
(Detect, Debate, Discriminate)

This may sound complicated or like a lot of work, and sometimes it is. But the alternative is to have negative feelings, a negative self-perception, and a negative outlook. For many, this process is already occurring in therapy groups and 12-step meetings. Sponsors, therapists, and peers in the meetings are challenging cognitive distortions. Alcoholics Anonymous (AA) calls cognitive distortions "stinking thinking." Its members challenge each other's thoughts when the thoughts are dysfunctional. The goal is to help addicts begin to challenge their distortions on their own.

The diagram below uses an example applied to the formula:

A The Activating Event	B Beliefs/Thoughts	C Consequences (emotional/behavioral)
Therapist speaking of members headed for a relapse.	*Therapist is talking about me.*	*Fear, isolation*
	I am headed for a relapse.	*Worry, anxiety*
	Why does the therapist think that?	*Confusion, defensiveness, resentment*
	I'm not working hard enough.	*Giving up, hurt, anger*
	I should be doing better.	*Self-deprecation*
	The therapist doesn't know what she is talking about.	*Embarrassment, dropping out of group/treatment, relapse*
	I'm no good.	*Feelings of self-pity.*

As you can see, if not handled appropriately, these thoughts can lead to negative behavior and possibly severe consequences. Now to demonstrate the cognitive challenges:

D Disputing Intervention Detect, Debate, Discriminate	E Effective Philosophy	F New Feelings
Detect: Is it possible I am thinking in a distorted fashion? **Possible distortions: personalizing, hypersensitivity, magnification/ exaggeration, arbitrary inference (catastrophizing)**	*I am doing what I need to do. I am not in imminent danger of relapse.*	*Confident, distortions– inquisitive*
Debate: Where is my evidence? Did the therapist address me individually? I am doing what needs to be done, attending meetings, working with a sponsor, completing all assignments, sharing. The therapist is making eye contact with a lot of people; perhaps it is a public speaking technique. The therapist does know what they are talking about; I have a lot of evidence to support that belief.	*If I am still confused, I can ask the therapist individually. The therapist is not identifying me. Other group members are not taking recovery seriously.*	*Calm, better self-image.*

The most difficult part is applying this process when caught up in dysfunctional belief systems. Often, dysfunctional beliefs are held onto with steadfast determination, despite their causing harm.

Another aspect of cognitive challenging is **reframing**. Reframing involves looking at the situation and finding the positives in it, despite first viewing it in a negative fashion. For example, a sponsor gives the client a tough assignment she does not want to do and doesn't see the benefit in. Reframing would be identifying how the assignment might be positive, having faith in the sponsor knowing what might help, and doing her best at it.

The reason cognitive challenging is so essential is easy to understand. Addiction is a disease that distorts reality. When in denial (and most in recovery can easily identify some examples of when they were), the substance user believed an alternative reality to others. He or she cannot see substance use as a problem, despite the abundance of evidence.

Addiction is often compared to the disease of diabetes. Although this is a valid analogy, the disease of addiction can more accurately be compared to a disease that affects thinking, such as schizophrenia. Most people are aware that when someone suffers with certain types of schizophrenia, they have delusions. Someone with paranoid schizophrenia may believe they are being followed and may have evidence, such as the fact that there always seems to be someone around outside on a cell phone. Those thinking rationally know that people on cell phones is not evidence of being followed. An addict who was arrested for drug use, lost his job because of absenteeism, and whose family is in conflict as a result of his substance use may still deny that substances are the problem. Is this so different from believing people on cell phones are following you? Charles Baudelaire once wrote something to the effect of "the Devil's greatest accomplishment was convincing the world he didn't exist." The same could be said of addiction: "Addiction's greatest accomplishment is convincing the addict that drugs are not the problem."

Challenging thinking often sounds either extremely complicated or overly simple to those entering recovery. In a way, it is both. It is simple because the logic makes complete sense: because one is involved in the situation, one loses objectivity. Regaining objectivity and looking at it rationally make perfect sense for better decision-making. Additionally, when one is hearing this explained or reading about it, one is not emotionally invested in the situation and is therefore able to see things more rationally. The difficulty comes in applying it when caught up in the thinking.

Cognitive challenging seems difficult to some because of the terms used and the thought that a formula needs to be learned and applied. Another reason it seems difficult is because many go through their day without paying much attention to their thoughts. Many people trust their way of thinking more than they put trust in anything else. This is not completely unfounded. But when a mental health issue is present, it clouds one's thinking and alters perception.

John, a 42-year-old biracial male, sought treatment after his seventh DUI. (Although today this would be unlikely to happen, this happened over a decade ago, and many of John's DUIs occurred when there was more tolerance for drinking and driving.) John did not believe he needed treatment. What's more, he didn't believe he had a drinking problem! He had an explanation for each and every DUI, and none were his fault. His explanations included not driving but being in possession of the keys and in the car (he had a flat, was bringing a bottle to a friend's house, and when broken down, decided to drink it while awaiting help). Another time, John had been drinking but was driving fine and another motorist hit him. Another DUI was given by a police officer who held a personal grudge against him and watched and waited for him to leave a drinking establishment. According to this client, bad luck and the malice of others led to his DUIs, not his drinking. In treatment, John was challenged to question his thinking and was eventually able to see that his "excuses" had been perpetuating his behavior.

The first step in applying these aforementioned techniques is to become aware of one's thinking. Therapists and counselors often begin this stage with the newly recovering individual by challenging his thinking for him. If the individual is not in therapy, a 12-step program will also provide this challenging. And if someone is not involved in either of these, he must look for some sort of mentor or trusted individual to help him give a reality test on his perceptions. It is really difficult to question your own thinking and begin trusting another. But although difficult, it is a crucial step to recovery.

In a less drastic example heard many times in early recovery, newly recovering individuals will be working a good program. They will be abstinent for some time and attending 12-step meetings. Often, they start looking better, putting on weight if it was needed, and generally giving off a more positive energy. They will then decide that now would be a good time to go back to their old using friends—just to show them how good they are doing. And in what is more evident of cognitive distortions, they will be thinking of this and not discuss the thoughts with their counselor or 12-step peers. They believe they already know what others will say (fortune-telling, but they may even be right) and they don't want to hear the feedback. Then they make the decision to visit, and this often leads to a relapse. The thought that it is a good idea to show using drug/alcohol buddies how good you are doing is irrational. It puts the individual in a risky situation and often leads to bad results. Interestingly, if they return to treatment, many will easily admit that it was a bad idea. They wonder what they were thinking. Thus, teaching them to recognize these thoughts and the appropriate responses to them can help individuals avoid these situations altogether.

The goal of early recovery, then, is to recognize that one has an addiction and to realize that it affects his thinking. Then the next step is to monitor the individual's thinking so as to identify distortions therein. In late recovery, the results of this pay off. When thoughts that are distorted occur, the individual has the ability to laugh them off. But, as mentioned, thoughts of substance use will likely occur for the recovering individual for the rest of his life.

Mindfulness-Based Therapies

For the last several years, the field of psychology has seen a shift toward Eastern philosophy—specifically, toward mindfulness and acceptance as a way to treat many psychological disorders. This movement has claimed and supported the benefit of mindfulness and meditation to individuals' mental health (Spijkerman, Pots, and Bohlmeijer, 2016). Many call these mindfulness and acceptance-based therapies the third wave of behaviorism (behaviorism was the first wave, cognitive behaviorism was the second). **Mindfulness** has been an Eastern technique since before the written word. Religions and philosophies that utilize and purport the importance of mindfulness include Buddhism and Taoism, as well as their offspring, Zen Buddhism. Now, while it is not our purpose to convert anyone to these religions or philosophies, there is great benefit in the use of the mindfulness techniques for improving one's mood and state of mind, and thus, behavior. Furthermore, these practices can vastly improve the techniques discussed in earlier the chapter on challenging thinking. The most common mindfulness-based therapies are dialectical behavioral therapy (**DBT**), acceptance and commitment therapy (**ACT**), and mindfulness-based cognitive therapy (**MBCT**). Interestingly, these third-wave therapies may serve as an excellent bridge between the first tier of addiction treatment (challenging thinking) and what is described in Chapter 6 as the pull phase of recovery (Helgoe, 2002) and would be considered more in line with depth psychology.

MBCT grew from the combination of cognitive therapy (CT) and mindfulness-based stress reduction (MBSR), which was developed by Jon Kabat-Zinn. The developers of MBCT, Segal, Williams, and Teasdale, had been practicing cognitive therapy and were trained in MBSR. The combination led to the formulation of MBCT for depression. One of the most important differences between CT and MBCT is that the focus is not challenging dysfunctional thinking (as in CT), but to allow not only thoughts but feelings and sensations as well and view them in a welcoming fashion (Segal, Williams, & Teasdale, 2013).

DBT was founded by Marsha Linehan in the 1990s as the treatment for borderline personality disorder, and since then, it has been adapted for substance abuse and eating disorders (Kahl, Winter, & Schweiger, 2012). DBT is a very structured treatment, and trainings are available to become certified in it.

Steven C. Hayes is credited with developing acceptance and commitment therapy (ACT). ACT attempts to help the client achieve their goals through six facets (acceptance, cognitive defusion, being present, self as context, values, and committed action) which result in psychological flexibility (Dixon, Wilson, & Habib, 2016). **Psychological flexibility** is attained through focusing on the present, acceptance of the internal and external experience, perceiving the self in context (the ability to step out of the situation and view oneself more objectively), and a term ACT calls **defusion**, which is nonattachment to thoughts, feelings, and sensations. Value exploration and commitment to the determined values rounds out the process.

There is often a lot of mystery centered on mindfulness, Eastern philosophy, and meditation. Meditation is often as simple as the practice of mindfulness. What is often heard from clients or peers when meditation is discussed is that they are not good at it. In reality no one is good at meditation, especially in the beginning. (Well, the Dalai Lama probably is.) Meditation can be difficult despite the simplicity of its nature. After all, it is simply the practice of monitoring your thoughts. If sitting to meditate, it is suggested you have your back straight, as certain positions are more able to remind you of your purpose and help you stay focused. However, as long as you're focusing on your thoughts, you can be flexible with your posture. Once sitting, it is often suggested that you imagine your mind as a blank movie screen. From that point on, you simply watch your thoughts appear and disappear from the screen.

Now this sounds simple, but it is often very difficult to apply. It is our nature to follow these thoughts and entertain them. This happens automatically; thoughts take on a life of their own. The mindfulness, or awareness of but separation from what one is thinking, is lost, and consciousness has now drifted away in other thoughts. It is the mind's nature to drift. Even the most experienced meditators' minds drift. The goal with meditation

FIGURE 4.3. Mindfulness-based relapse prevention incorporates mindfulness-based cognitive therapy for depression and stress reduction techniques, which decreases relapse rates when compared to treatment as usual (Bowen et al., 2014).

is to catch this game in action, come back to the breath or a chant or to the blank screen, and simply watch the thoughts again.

Most people who try but give up on meditation explain it is difficult to maintain focus on the breath and simply watch their thoughts. But again, this is natural. Everyone's mind wanders. In meditation, the meditator is returning to a deeper state, where thoughts are born. It is difficult to maintain this focus on the breath. That is okay; it is normal. It is the practice of meditation that brings more success. More success is simply catching the wandering mind faster and maintaining focus longer. There is no perfection in meditation. The practice of watching your thoughts in and of itself brings a more objective view of them. And with this objective view comes more peace, and less acting on impulse, than consciously thinking the situation through.

Mindfulness is the result of this practice. It increases the ability to be aware of thinking while being somewhat detached from it. It is recognizing that thoughts are simply thoughts—not truths, not demands for action (this is described as *defusion* in ACT). Meditation helps bring about mindfulness. And mindfulness helps bring about better decision-making. This can be unparalleled in its benefit to addiction recovery (as well as many other dilemmas). Once an individual has navigated mindfulness, action or acceptance based on what was noticed is a natural next step.

There are often mixed reactions to the idea of **acceptance**. Some feel it is resignation and view it in a negative sense. It is not, however, negative. Probably the best definition about radical acceptance comes from Jon Kabat Zinn, who has written numerous books on the subject:

> *Acceptance doesn't, by any stretch of the imagination, mean passive resignation. Quite the opposite. It takes a huge amount of fortitude and motivation to accept what is—especially when you don't like it—and then work wisely and effectively as best you possibly can with the circumstances you find yourself in and with the resources at your disposal, both inner and outer, to mitigate, heal, redirect, and change what can be changed. (2005, p. 407)*

Acceptance is a cornerstone in Buddhist thought. There are Four Noble Truths in Buddhism, the second of which focuses on acceptance: "Desire is the root of all suffering." In Buddhist teaching, suffering occurs when we wish things to be different than they are. Simply, wanting one's experience of the world to be different than it is leads to suffering and demonstrates a lack of acceptance (Berry, 2015). There is a saying that reflects this: Pain is inevitable, suffering is optional.

Acceptance is about accepting situations as they are without wishing for them to be different. However, when used appropriately, acceptance allows us to work toward positive change, without judgment or other negative thoughts and feelings.

Acceptance has been a central component of the 12-step process (which much of addiction treatment is based on) since its inception. An excellent passage showing the connection between acceptance and the 12-step process can be found in the book *Alcoholics Anonymous*, which AA members refer to as "the Big Book." It was written by Paul Ohliger (1939) and states

> *acceptance is the answer to all my problems today. When I am disturbed, it is because I find some person, place, thing, or situation-some fact of my life-unacceptable to me, and can find no serenity until I accept that person, place, thing or situation as being exactly the way it is supposed to be at this moment. Nothing, absolutely nothing, happens in God's world by mistake.*
>
> *Unless I accept life completely on life's terms, I cannot be happy. I need to concentrate not so much on what needs to be changed in the world, as on what needs to be changed in me and in my attitudes.*
> (Alcoholics Anonymous, 4th ed., 2013, p. 417)

Noticeably religious in nature, a more concise description of practicing acceptance would be difficult to find (Berry, 2017). Meditation, too, has also been a part of the 12-step process since its beginning, and it also folds in religious undertones. One can deduce that most religions include a level of meditation, mindfulness, and acceptance based on their doctrines and practices. Therefore, the recovery process, when utilizing a mindfulness approach, lends itself to finding and sitting with a higher power. For example, the 11th step in Alcoholics Anonymous mentions seeking, through meditation, the improvement of one's relationship with a higher power. The second-highest-selling book related to AA, *The 24 Hour a Day Book* by Richard Walker, published in 1954, includes meditations for each day. The fact it was written in 1954, long before meditation and mindfulness became psychology buzzwords, and that it is the number two selling book related to Alcoholics Anonymous, is a clear testament to the popularity and success mindfulness has had on the recovery process (Berry, 2017).

Summary

Cognitions are a critical area to analyze when working with the substance use disorder population. However, to even broach the thought process, the addict must push past his denial for the recovery process to begin. Ultimately, how a person thinks greatly influences his behavior, and an addict needs to accept their thinking process is distorted by addiction in order to recover. The founder of cognitive therapy, Aaron Beck, spearheaded the understanding of thought. This led to many theorists developing models to target specific populations. Abraham Twerski and Terence Gorski are two notable theorists in the addiction field. Both have established theories that have launched many successful recovery programs. As the field of addiction evolves, mindfulness-based practices are establishing a legitimate mark. Mindfulness-based therapies, specifically, can be wonderful assets to addiction recovery, as well as helping with other psychological issues (Kabat-Zinn, 2005; Kahl, Winter, & Schweiger, 2012; Bowen et al., 2014; Dixon, Wilson, & Habib, 2016). Mindfulness separates one from his or her thoughts and allows one to step back and recognize the difference between thinking arising from addictive tendencies and healthier thinking. Acceptance occurs when the present moment is perceived in a nonjudgmental way (Berry, 2015) and when thoughts about what should be (an irrational belief in rational emotive behavioral therapy (REBT) are quelled and put aside. Meditation isn't as mysterious as it sounds, and the practice is what is beneficial, not the perfection of it. Simply sitting quietly and observing your thoughts is an excellent method to confront addiction and assist in recovery. Through combining cognitive behavior therapy techniques and mindfulness practices, the addiction population is benefiting from a more holistic approach to treatment.

Key Terms

Cognitive distortions	CBT	DBT
Denial	Euphoric recall	ACT
Hypersensitivity	Positive expectancy	
Personalizing	Trigger event	
Fortune-telling	Obsession	
False sense of entitlement	Compulsion	
	Craving	
Projection	Activating event	
Catastrophizing	Detect, Debate, Discriminate	
Fear of emotion		
Minimizing	Reframing	
Rationalization	Mindfulness	
Justifying	Defusion	
Cognitive	Acceptance	
CT	MBCT	

CHAPTER FIVE

12-Step Sober and Other Support Groups

Learning Objectives

- Identify different 12-step meetings and the issues they address.
- Discuss the similarities and differences between some of the 12-step groups.
- Refer a potential client to the appropriate 12-step meeting.
- Explain the protocol of 12-step groups.
- Explain the benefits of 12-step meetings.
- Describe the role of sponsorship in meetings
- Discuss the drawbacks of 12-step meetings.
- Identify other sober support groups that do not follow the 12-step format.

Introduction

Although there is controversy regarding **12-step sober support groups,** studies indicate clinically meaningful benefit and affordability resulting from AA participation (Kelly, 2017). 12-step groups are an integral part of addiction treatment. The first 12-step support group, **Alcoholics Anonymous**, was founded in 1935 by Bill Wilson and Bob Smith. The premise is that one alcoholic/addict can best help another, and that by helping another, you actually help yourself. Freely helping one another is the premise of AA, NA, CA, OA, and any other 12-step program in existence.

Since the inception of 12-step meetings in 1935 with just two members, AA has mushroomed into 118,000 groups with over two million members in 180 countries (Alcoholics Anonymous World Services, 2018). There are 12-step meetings for many different problems, and even within one group

FIGURE 5.1. All 12-step support groups use the template of the same 12 steps. These steps focus on personal and spiritual growth.

(Narcotics Anonymous, for example) there are many types of meetings (step meetings, speaker meetings, meditation meetings, etc.). These meetings are different in ways, but similar in their main objective: helping the recovering person overcome their addiction.

Twelve-step meetings can be daunting to the newly recovering individual. Many have distaste for the religious doctrine and dogma present. There is a reference to "God" or "Higher Power" in six of the 12 steps. And there is a moral tone in many of the others.

For individuals who have had a bad experience with God or religion, they might never return to the 12-step model. We have often heard new clients report that the meetings were like a cult. Some hate the prayers, which are Christian or Judeo-Christian. Some have reported feeling like everyone was brainwashed. Brainwashing carries a very negative connotation, as if you have no control over your thinking. But as we saw in the earlier chapter, challenging thinking and learning to think differently about problems can completely alter one's life. In fact, it is a way to gain more control over your thinking, as the distortions common to substance use have significantly less effect on the addict's thinking. The 12-step program is a very efficient way to aid in these changes in thinking.

Types of 12-Step Support Groups

Alcoholics Anonymous (AA)

As previously mentioned, the first 12-step support group was Alcoholics Anonymous. These groups can range from two to 200 people, with meetings taking place in most cities and many towns throughout the United States and many other countries. Each support group has a set of officers from the membership who are elected or volunteer every six months. The **chairperson** opens and closes the meetings; this person is typically a veteran of the 12 steps. The **treasurer** manages all funds and donations. The **secretary** makes announcements and organizes the meetings.

The perception of Alcoholics Anonymous is that it is only for individuals who are ready to join. This is not the case. There are two types of meetings: open and closed. An **open meeting** is as the name implies; it is a meeting that welcomes all who are interested. This meeting will usually have speakers with a minimum of 90 days sobriety. **Closed meetings, however, are limited** to those who have officially joined. Joining, however, simply means the individual admits he/she has the issue the meeting addresses. These meetings remain closed in order to respect the anonymity of the members.

What occurs in a meeting can range from discussing the steps to qualifications. **Qualifications** are the stories a speaker will share that describe his use, journey, and consequences. When an individual is seeking to explore AA as an option, it is recommended that she or he attend a **beginners' meeting**. This meeting is designed to address the skills needed in early recovery. Famous slogans are typically used in these meetings, such as "It's the first drink that gets you drunk"; "Easy does it"; and "First things first." The most powerful piece of a beginners' meeting is a new member realizing that he is not alone in his struggle.

A.A. World Services, Inc.
475 Riverside Drive at West 120th St., 11th Floor
New York, NY 10115
(212) 870-3400
www.aa.org

Carlos is a 19-year-old Hispanic male who has struggled with alcohol abuse since he was 14. He began individual psychotherapy at the age of 18 and attended irregularly. Carlos' therapist struggled as she worked with him. She expressed the importance of his attending AA as an adjunct to individual treatment. However, Carlos had myriad excuses each time why he didn't want to go (e.g., "I don't connect"; "There's no one my age"; "Those people are really messed up"). His therapist didn't want to abandon him by setting attendance to AA as a contingency to individual treatment, so she continued to see him on and off for a year and a half. When Carlos turned 19 and his drinking was preventing him from following through with his daily responsibilities, his therapist involved his family. She explained to them the limitations of treatment when AA is not an adjunct. Because attending groups was becoming a reality, Carlos finally admitted that the reason why he didn't want to go to the groups was because everyone else had their drinking under control and he couldn't even get there. With that, his therapist realized that Carlos wasn't going to a beginners' group. After a beginners' group was located, Carlos began attending the meetings and is now a strong advocate for them.

Cocaine Anonymous (CA)

Cocaine Anonymous is a 12-step support group that has a similar format to AA. It began in Los Angeles in 1982 and was founded by a member of AA. In addition to following the 12 steps, CA members are advised to "throw away all your drug paraphernalia and drugs; don't deal and if your connection calls, hang up" (Straussner, 2014). In addition, the use of any other mind-altering substances is discouraged. Those who experience crack addiction are also able to participate in this fellowship. The meetings are structured similarly to those of AA. The speakers share their experiences of using the substance, the negative consequences, and how their recovery is proceeding. A common feeling experienced by most cocaine/crack users is that of apathy. Sharing this with others brings a sense of universality.

CAWSO
21720 S. Wilmington Ave., Ste. 304
Long Beach, CA 90810-1641
310-559-5833
www.ca.org

Narcotics Anonymous (NA)

Narcotics Anonymous was founded in 1953 and is the second largest 12-step support group. It is modeled after AA and was developed as a society of men and women who simply want to stop using drugs because it has become a problem for them. In 1978, there were less than 200 groups in three countries; in 2000, there were 28,207 meetings held weekly in 104 countries. In 2016, there were nearly 67,000 weekly meetings held throughout 139 countries (Narcotics Anonymous World Services, 2016).

Narcotics Anonymous considers "addiction" the issue and not a specific drug. The 12 steps are amended slightly from AA to accommodate this thinking. For example, Step 1 in NA is "We admitted that we were powerless over our addiction, that our lives had become unmanageable." The slogan is "Take people, not a hit," and the only requirement to attend is the desire to stop using. Similar to AA, there are both open and closed groups. Narcotics Anonymous is very passionate about newcomers and feels they are the most important persons in the meetings.

NA World Services
PO Box 9999
Van Nuys, CA 91409
818-773-9999
www.na.org

Dual Recovery Anonymous (DRA)

Dual Recovery Anonymous is a 12-step support group that was founded in Kansas in 1989 and, like other support groups, was adapted from AA. This group is intended for those who have been struggling with emotional and psychiatric illness as well as addiction. What is different about this group is that in order to treat the psychiatric illness, many members may be using prescription medication (this may be frowned upon in other 12-step meetings such as AA). Also, this group focuses on learning how to reduce the symptoms of mental illness, as well as developing relapse prevention skills. This population is particularly challenging because the mental illness and chemical dependency are enmeshed. Often, the substance use helps to minimize the psychiatric symptoms. Therefore, once the substance use has ceased, the psychiatric symptoms will increase, leading the person back to the substance to cope. This is the premise behind explaining to members that attending meetings is not a substitute for treatment.

Dual Recovery Anonymous
World Network Central Office
PO Box 8107
Prairie Village, KS 66208
1-877-883-2332
www.draonline.org

AL-ANON/Alateen, aka AL-ANON Family Groups

AL-ANON is the world's largest support group for friends and families of alcoholics. Historically, these meetings developed in the kitchens of the homes of those in AA as the spouses gathered to prepare coffee and cakes. Specifically, it was founded by Lois Wilson, wife of Bill Wilson (founder of AA) in 1951. **Alateen**, serving the population aged 13–19, began in 1957. The majority of the members of AL-ANON Family Groups are female, and the slogan is "I didn't cause alcoholism, I can't control it, and I can't cure it." This group also follows the 12-step culture.

AL-ANON Family Group Headquarters
1600 Corporate Landing Pkwy
Virginia Beach, VA 23454
757-563-1600
www.al-anon.alateen.org

Benefits

There are many benefits to attending 12-step meetings. One is a feeling of **camaraderie**. Camaraderie is a feeling of belonging, acceptance, and the sharing of a common pain. It is often used in reference to war and comrades-in-arms. But many who attend 12-step meetings experience this feeling and discuss how it benefits them. Substance users often feel misunderstood and as if no one "gets them." Twelve-step meetings frequently provide a much-lacking sense of belonging.

Moreover, meta analyses suggest that the benefits of AA occur through multiple mechanisms simultaneously—specifically, through facilitating adaptive social network changes and by boosting self-efficacy (Kelly, 2017). Simply, attending 12-step meetings provides a more positive social network, and in all likelihood, that bolsters the belief one can stay sober and improves one's mood.

Another benefit of being involved in 12-step programs is the 12 steps themselves. The 12 steps, when worked with honesty, help many people with addictions to stay sober/clean and grow emotionally. Additionally, addiction recovery is often described as requiring a program of personal and spiritual growth. The 12 steps provide the vehicle for this growth, and to some, the formula for **enlightenment** and **self-actualization**, which will be discussed later in this book.

An additional benefit of 12-step groups is the idea of **sponsorship**. A sponsor is a mentor, someone who has been in recovery for more than a year, and who is willing to help a newcomer attain and maintain recovery. This individual usually guides the newcomer through the 12 steps. He also provides sober support and an emergency contact in some cases. Many sponsors tell their **sponsees**, "Call me anytime, and always call before you pick up that first drink."

For some people entering recovery, 12-step meetings can provide activity. When one gives up substances and its surrounding activities, there may be large periods of time left vacant in one's day. Attending meetings puts activity in a person's day and can detract from boredom.

Joining a home group is another benefit inherent in 12-step meetings. A home group is a meeting that is joined because it is found to be the most comfortable meeting for that person. The individual then gets to know many of the other members, participates in business meetings for the group, and gets involved in decision-making for the group.

Finally, as the philosophy of the program states, one stays sober by freely giving away his experience, strength, and hope to a newcomer. Many of our clients have said when they've progressed in recovery that seeing someone coming in and struggling helps "**keep it green**" for them. This refers to remembering what it was like to struggle to remain abstinent and refreshing the memory that one doesn't want to go back that place.

As addiction therapists, we are aware of the benefits available through 12-step attendance. We encourage everyone to attend a few meetings before deciding it is not for him or her. There are many benefits in the groups, and if the substance user can get past whatever distaste he might have, he will likely reap these benefits. But we also understand many who recover do so without 12-step involvement.

Our advice to any client who is vehemently against 12-step involvement is to then develop a program for personal and spiritual growth as well as sober support—that he will stick to. This might be reading material related to addiction, personal growth, and spirituality. It might be getting involved in some type of ongoing therapy. It might simply be returning to church and participating in more than just services. In addition to a program of growth, the individual will benefit from increasing his sober support. This sober support must include someone who understands addiction. Many who have never had an addiction don't understand when people say "I feel like using" after they've been abstinent a while. This is difficult to grasp when things have seemingly become so much better. When the support is a family member or loved one, this might also trigger fear in them, increasing the chance they will not react objectively. The person unfamiliar with substance addiction will generally react negatively to news that the addict is thinking of using. This can further exacerbate the problem. But someone in addiction recovery understands this statement and the thoughts and feelings associated with it, and can usually relate and not react negatively.

Sponsorship

A **sponsor** is generally a same-sex sober person who has successfully worked the 12 steps. The role of a sponsor is to provide guidance and mentorship to a newcomer as he works toward sobriety. According to the 2014 AA membership survey of over 8,000 members in the United States and Canada, 82% of members have a sponsor and 74% got a sponsor within 90 days (Alcoholics Anonymous World Services, 2012, p. 48). The sponsor relationship is critical in helping the newcomer work through feelings of despair and isolation. Often, newcomers will drop out of support groups because they feel they don't connect with others. Many times, it takes the mentorship of a sponsor to help the person make a connection to others.

The idea of sponsorship brings us to the next benefit: sober support. Members of the 12-step program provide each other with their phone numbers. Additionally, new friendships can be formed, and members can help each other remain sober in and out of meetings.

Drawbacks

We are not saying everyone who will be supportive has to be in recovery. There are two types of sober support: those who are in recovery and can relate, and those who are supportive because they care about the substance user.

Our suggestion is that newly recovering individuals have plenty of both. But if 12-step meetings are out of the question for them, they should find someone who can relate to their issue. With the Internet being what it is today, supportive relationships can be found in online support groups as well. There is even a social network website for those in addiction recovery called In the Rooms. Most 12-step support groups also have online meetings.

A further complication with 12-step meetings is that many programs mandate attendance. Although this can have benefits (some who attend due to being mandated come to embrace the program), it can also have drawbacks. Some people use their manipulative and deception skills to convince others they are going to meetings when they are not. The fact they are mandated can also bring about defiance in many clients who are rebellious to authority.

Mark, an 18-year-old Puerto Rican male, began attending AA two months ago. His parents were very pleased because Mark would leave Monday, Wednesday, and Friday each week at 7:30 p.m. to make it to the 8:00 p.m. meeting at a local community church. Mark's parents expressed to him how proud they are of him and that they look forward to his three-months-sober chip. Mark left the discussion with his parents feeling broken. He had been lying to them the past month about attending the meetings. He stopped going because one month into the meeting he arrived late and was chastised (so he felt) by another member. The reality was the other member simply mentioned that he should try to arrive on time. Mark's exaggerated interpretation of the interaction caused him to have a slip. He didn't want to feel like he was being "watched" or "tracked." Mark finally admitted to his parents what happened and agreed to go to meetings, but at a different location.

Another concern people have with 12-step groups is the focus on God. For many who do not subscribe to a religion, this deters participation. Many groups have made recommendations to consider God as an acronym for "**Good Orderly Direction**." Despite the original religious undergirding of the 12 steps, the majority of 12-step officers recognize this limitation and encourage members to see this theme as merely a guide and not a rule. It is more important to focus on the intention of the step rather than the religious implication.

Some feel that attending meetings can become addictive in and of itself. In a way, people view the meetings as a substitute for the chemical addiction. Using Alcoholics Anonymous as the litmus for most support groups, members attend an average of 2.5 meetings per week, according to the 2014 AA Membership

Survey. What does occur is an increased number of meetings attended per week when someone is beginning his journey of sobriety. As the person gains greater control of their sobriety, there is a natural diminishing of attendance. However, there are those who do continue to attend meetings frequently and regularly. These individuals may be using the meetings as a way to cope or self-medicate. If this is the case, it may be considered a harmless alternative to substances while still reflecting a need for additional counseling.

Another criticism of 12-step support groups is the rule of complete abstinence. This is an approach that might not necessarily work for everyone. **Harm reduction**, which involves slowly reducing the amount of use and resulting negative consequences, is another treatment approach and is discussed later in this text. The premise behind harm reduction is that each person achieves sobriety at a different pace. For some, it is either too difficult or painful to abstain completely. These individuals opt for a harm reduction route in order to minimize the likelihood of relapse. Although 12-step groups speak of abstinence as the goal, the only true requirement is the desire to stop use. The members are not policed or tested to see if they are using. However, it is in the culture to at least want to completely abstain.

Many professionals take issue with the beginning stages of the 12-step philosophy: First, the "acceptance of powerlessness" runs counter to therapeutic ideals. (The first step of the 12-step process is admitting powerlessness over the addiction). Second, a person needs to go to meetings for the rest of his life. Although these points are valid, there can be an alternate way of viewing them. With regard to 12-step meeting attendance being lifelong, members who continue attendance generally do so not out of obligation but out of believing it benefits them and from feeling a sense of community. They are not pushed into going as much as wanting to do so (a theory of recovery regarding the push phase and pull phase of recovery will be discussed in Chapter 6).

With regard to the idea of powerlessness being a negative, we offer a more **existential approach.** Earlier in the text we stated that the first tier of addiction treatment is cognitive. Although the first step of a 12-step program may not be beyond the first tier, concepts related to it are. Typical psychotherapy has empowerment as a goal. The client should realize his power and his choices, and feel as if he is more in control of his life. Despite the seeming paradox, when one admits he does not have control of something, he gains more control in his life. Understanding one's weakness gives one power. In existential therapy, it is a challenge to the client to accept that one has less control in life than believed, that the universe is uncaring and chaotic, that bad things happen to good people. In a sense, one is challenged to accept powerlessness in life but to own the power he has. This may seem a bit complicated and paradoxical, but as stated in *Twelve Steps and Twelve Traditions*, "It is only through utter defeat are we able to take our first steps toward liberation and strength. Our admissions of our personal powerlessness finally turn out to be firm bedrock on which happy and purposeful lives may be built" (Alcoholics Anonymous, 1981, p. 21). By realizing one's weakness, by accepting what one does not have power over, one is able to plan accordingly.

As a therapist, it is significant to encourage clients to explore new behaviors that may assist them in their goal of abstinence. At the same time, it is critical to meet clients where they are in their recovery process, with the intention of encouraging further movement. Mandating 12-step attendance can work against the therapeutic rapport.

The preceding paragraphs attempt to give a balanced summary of 12-step programs. There are benefits, there are drawbacks, and there might be benefit in some of the drawbacks. As we hope you have garnered from the text thus far, there is no one way to treat addiction. As the master therapist Irvin Yalom suggests, the therapist should "strive to create a new therapy for each patient" (Yalom, 2002, p. 34).

In Appendix B, there is a 12-step assignment sheet we use with clients.

Other Support Groups for Addiction

There are several other groups that offer support for the cessation of addiction. One is a Christian version of the 12-step programs, called **Celebrate Recovery**. Two other groups, **SMART Recovery** and **Refuge Recovery**, differ from the 12-step approach significantly.

Celebrate Recovery is generally held in and organized by the church. It usually begins with a sermon, followed by smaller groups focusing on specific issues (having an addiction, having a partner who is an addict) that meet in different areas of the church. It began in 1991 in California. It is now in over 35,000 churches and has recently spread to recovery houses, prisons, and universities (Celebrate Recovery, 2018).

SMART stands for Self-Management and Recovery Training. SMART Recovery began in 1994, and according to their 2016 Annual Report, they have 2,149 meetings (SMART Recovery, 2016). The groups are led by a volunteer who is trained in some cognitive behavioral interventions for addiction. These differ from 12-step meetings in that they are run by members with no training. "SMART Recovery's mission is to offer donation-requested, self-empowering, science-based, face-to-face and online support groups for abstaining from any substance or activity addiction" (SMART Recovery, 2018). SMART Recovery differs from the 12-step programs in that there is no religious or spiritual aspect; members are taught tools to help them remain abstinent (or become abstinent) and receive support and shared experiences with the group.

Refuge Recovery is a support group for those desiring to overcome any addiction. They base their program on the Four Truths of Recovery and the Eightfold Path (both adopted from Buddhism). Meetings generally have meditation to start the session, and mindfulness (discussed in Chapter 4) is an integral part of the recovery program (Refuge Recovery, 2018).

Summary

There are pros and cons to being involved in a 12-step program for recovery. Some view it as another form of dependence. Others believe it a necessity to a sustained, fruitful recovery and any semblance of happiness in the life of the recovering individual. Twelve-step meetings are neither a savior, as many make them out to be, nor a cult, as others contend. Twelve-step meetings offer many benefits, and there are drawbacks. The fact that many rehabilitation centers require 12-step attendance may be an indicator of its benefit, or as many contend (Dodes, 2002; Peele, 1985), it has simply become institutionalized in the field of addiction treatment despite evidence many cease addictive use without using or continuing 12-step attendance.

Not everyone in a 12-step program is working a good program, and the maxim "Progress, Not Perfection" allows for individuals to make mistakes, be miserable at times, and otherwise fall short of the ideals of the program. This does not mean the program doesn't work for many. At the same time, it isn't for everyone. Twelve-step meetings often have a culture all their own, and it is best for someone entering addiction recovery to try several before drawing a definitive conclusion.

There are also alternative support groups for recovery that have been growing in popularity. These include Celebrate Recovery, SMART Recovery, and Refuge Recovery. Although they have some similarities to the 12-step approach (group meetings, support for abstinence) they differ greatly in other ways and offer alternatives to those uncomfortable with the traditional 12-step approach.

Key Terms

12-step sober support groups	Chairperson	Open meeting
Alcoholics Anonymous	Treasurer	Closed meetings
	Secretary	Qualifications

Beginners' meeting
Cocaine Anonymous
Narcotics Anonymous
AL-ANON
Dual Recovery
  Anonymous
Alateen
Camaraderie

Enlightenment
Self-actualization
Sponsorship
Sponsee
Keep it green
Sponsor
Good Orderly
  Direction

Harm reduction
Celebrate Recovery
Existential approach
SMART Recovery
Refuge Recovery

CHAPTER SIX

The Recovery Process

Learning Objectives

- Discuss the phases of the recovery process.
- Explain the importance of changing associations, as well as how a counselor should approach reluctance to changing associations.
- Identify and discuss the stages of change.
- Explain the importance of clients identifying a theory as to why they became addicted.
- Describe how the stages of change relate to the recovery process.
- Explain post-acute withdrawal.
- Describe the "pink cloud," or "honeymoon," stage of recovery.
- Discuss some exercises that help the recovery process.
- Identify pitfalls inherent in each stage of the process of recovery.
- Describe the "push and pull phase" view of recovery.
- Discuss how the grieving process relates to addiction recovery.

Introduction

The recovery process assumes multiple relapses. However, it is crucial to accept those relapses as part of the recovery process rather than a failure of it. The core component of the recovery process is the recovering person's own internalized motivation. It is his motivation that will influence whether a recovering addict will relapse and, if so, how well he overcomes it. Miller and Rollnich (2002) identified essential elements to consider regarding motivation to change. Motivation to change often begins with the experience of distress caused by current behavior. That distress often fuels the individual to find alternative patterns

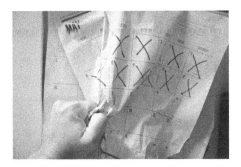

FIGURE 6.1. Although the recovery process assumes multiple relapses, it doesn't mean the recovering person has failed. The way one responds to setbacks in the recovery process is what is important.

of behavior that will alleviate or prevent future distress. In order to determine if one is ready for change, personal goals need to be considered. If the goal is only to reduce substance use and not eliminate it, then a more non-traditional, harm-reduction treatment intervention should be sought out (harm reduction will be discussed in a later chapter). However, if the individual has set the goal of eliminating substance use completely, then verbalizing and describing how valued that goal is will be essential. Outlining personal and familial gains to abstention often provide the foundation for how strongly a person values his goal.

There is a somewhat contradictory component to success in addiction recovery. On the one hand, self-confidence is essential to continued recovery but often difficult to establish. One must believe that he can function beneficially in society and contribute to his own well-being and the well-being of others. If a person is able to do so, his confidence will slowly be reinforced. For the small window of time before one tests his abilities, it is essential that he believes in himself. This leap of faith is a hallmark in addiction recovery. One must first believe that he can do it, do it, and then be glad that he did it.

On the other hand, overconfidence is highly correlated to relapse. Too many addicts trust their own thinking, do not listen to those providing guidance (such as their family, therapist, or 12-step group peers), and end up relapsing as a result. This is often a result of the thinking distortions discussed in Chapter 4, which culminate in denial or minimizing.

The Stages of Change

Often, the recovery process begins prior to actual abstinence. In their seminal work on the stages of change, or transtheoretical model of motivation, Prochaska, Norcross, and DiClemente (1994) identified five stages of change: As "a predictor of treatment initiation, adherence, and out-comes, motivation for change has received considerable attention within the substance abuse research field. Most notably evaluated within the framework of the Transtheoretical Model (TTM)" (Kushnir et al., 2016).

The transtheoretical model of motivation (or the stages of change model, as we prefer to call it) has been studied a great deal, with mixed results. Some studies indicate it is not effective or, at the least, that it is lacking (Panting, Swift, Goodman, & Davis, 2018; Bunton et al., 2000). However, the model continues to receive considerable consideration, and frankly, is very relatable. As such, your authors will continue to utilize it to explain the recovery process throughout this text.

The first stage is the **precontemplation stage**. At this point, the individual is not ready to consider a change at all. When Berry smoked cigarettes (and before he had ever heard of these stages of change), a supervisor asked him when he would quit smoking. He replied, "I like smoking. I have no intention of quitting." The supervisor replied, "Oh, you are in the precontemplation stage." In the case of those addicted to substances, who often enter treatment as a result of someone or something forcing them, this is an appropriate stage in which to start. The client sees no need to change and therefore is in the precontemplation stage.

Ryan is a 23-year-old African American male who smoked marijuana on a daily basis. He didn't want to stop, but it was hurting his family. They believed it was partly responsible for his social isolation, distance from the family, and depression. He spent the majority of his days and nights in his room with minimal interaction. During his course of treatment, Ryan was able to stop marijuana. However, he said that the thought of life without something to alter his mind was a wretched thought. He shared that he needed something to help cope with life. Ryan figured out a way to get around his family. He recognized that their issue was with using marijuana. So, Ryan began drinking, which was more socially acceptable in his home. Although Ryan was able to stop using marijuana, he substituted it with alcohol. He eventually discontinued treatment. Evidently, Ryan was in the contemplation stage of change. He recognized the issue and the negative consequence of using but was unwilling to accept his life without some form of substance use.

In the second stage, **contemplation**, the individual begins to think about change but is ambivalent, and he or she does not foresee change happening in the near future. In this case, the substance user may begin to realize there is a problem but doesn't believe change is possible or can't imagine a life without substances. The user might even answer friends or family members who say to the individual that he or she has a problem with "Yeah, so what?" For the

FIGURE 6.2. In the preparation stage of recovery, many try to cut down, change substances, or otherwise control their substance use.

substance user, at this moment, stopping isn't an option; the thought of a life without substances seems unbearable. This is thought to be true for most addicts.

For many of those who chronically use substances, it seems unimaginable to endure their existence without the aid of substances. One must remember that substances, for the addicted, have become the chief **coping mechanism**. A coping mechanism is a method with which an individual manages intolerable emotions related to stressors in the environment or triggers from within. You can imagine how you might feel if stripped of your most common coping mechanisms. Some substance-dependent individuals appear hostile. They are not angry currently, but they give the appearance that they are angry with life. They are looking for a sense of relief as they head for something they can rely on to deliver them from this state. At the contemplation stage, they may recognize there is a problem but can't imagine giving up the substance, as they rely on it to make life bearable. It is a sad state to be in, and as a therapist, one must have compassion for this and do his best to instill both hope and the belief that the individual can accomplish it.

The third stage is **preparation**. In this stage, individuals begin experimenting with some changes because they realize that change needs to occur. This realization has usually come about as a result of serious consequences resulting from substance use. The individual is now able to see that it is the substance that is the issue, albeit temporarily.

However, there is significant difficulty sustaining the desire to change. Perhaps the individual attempts to cut down their substance use or change substances for a time. Perhaps they change from liquor to beer, or rather than using cocaine or heroin, they only smoke marijuana (also known as **marijuana maintenance**). Other typical behaviors during this stage include pacing (drinking or using at a predetermined slower pace, like nursing a drink or drinking water between drinks); cutting down the amount of the substance used; only using during predesignated times (like only on weekends or only after 8:00 p.m.); changing the frequency of use; and lastly, temporary abstinence ("I won't use for a few weeks"). However, the individual is still hesitant about full abstention.

When we discuss the 12 steps of the AA or NA program with clients (which will be discussed more thoroughly later in the text), we emphasize that the first step is the only step necessary for abstinence. The first step is "We admitted we were powerless over our addiction and that our lives had become unmanageable." It is the other 11 steps that are geared at being happy without substances. Knowing one cannot use successfully anymore is sufficient to maintain abstinence. However, coming to that realization, and continuing to believe it, is difficult.

In the **action stage**, the person has committed to and achieved abstinence. Clear steps have been made toward the cessation of the substance use. Often, a person in this stage faces multiple relapses. However, their level of commitment drives them to resume abstention. The final stage is **maintenance**. Here the person has achieved sobriety for a sustained period of time (e.g., over a year). We will now turn the discussion to some of the helpful processes in the action stage.

On Early Change: Associations

Traditional addiction recovery requires abstinence from psychoactive drugs, *plus* change. It begins with the cessation of all psychoactive substance use and requires motivation to be internalized. Old friends, places, and habits are often left behind. This is usually a very difficult task for the newly recovering person. Some of these friends are from childhood. Some are the only people the addict felt comfortable with. There is often a strong bond, a feeling of camaraderie that seems unparalleled to the substance user. The thought of giving up not only his substance but his friends may seem overwhelming.

Still, many believe this is essential to sustaining recovery. It is very difficult to remain abstinent when those around you are using. Some people entering recovery will have friends willing to stop their substance use, at least around their friend who is stopping. Many might think this is fine and may continue the relationship. Although it is better than being with active users, it has its drawbacks as well. One drawback is that this friend is likely a **trigger**. (A *trigger* is a term used to describe a precipitator to increased

FIGURE 6.3. Recovery often requires one to change their friends and activities. New contacts are imperative as one lets go of those associated with substance use.

drug or alcohol thoughts, urges, or cravings.) Because the friend and drug use are so closely associated, it is likely just being with a friend who used will create at least thoughts of substance use in the recovering individual. Another example is if the newly recovering addict wants to use and is with his friend, a substance might be more readily accessible.

In a case that exemplifies the importance of individualizing a treatment plan, the client was a 21-year-old Caucasian male who was reluctant to give up his friends despite a strong commitment to abstinence. He continued to go to get-togethers with them and reported they did not have substance abuse issues but used socially. The client reported this didn't bother him. He said, in fact, that his friends didn't want to see him go down that path again and would not let him relapse with them. He remained abstinent despite continuing what many would consider risky relationships and finished treatment successfully without relapse at follow-up. In sessions, the therapist would occasionally address the risk factors with him, process any feelings when he was at a party with them, and explore the types of behaviors engaged in with these peers. This illuminated behaviors that the client recognized as contrary to recovery. Nonetheless, the client's will and determination guarded him against the influence of his peers.

This is a rare example, but it exemplifies how treatment must be individualized. Despite the risk, the client remained abstinent beyond treatment. Although it is easier to make generalized statements about how hanging with old friends will lead to relapse, clients must be responsible for the decisions they make and must feel free to discuss these decisions in therapy.

The fact is—and most substance users know this—one cannot completely avoid exposure to substances. However, one must consider the risk involved in maintaining unhealthy friendships. Fortunately, many of these friendships die as a result of the changes a recovering person makes. As someone progresses in recovery, his interests change, and these old friends often become obsolete. Frequently, the recovering individual recognizes that what he had in common, a similar perception of life and the enjoyment of substances, has changed. Hopefully, the recovering individual creates new, healthy relationships that replace the obsolete ones.

New relationships that promote personal growth must be developed to sustain ongoing recovery. Many people entering recovery forge these new relationships in **self-help support groups**. Others, while creating a new life for themselves, discover new friendships in new activities: returning to school, work or career changes, and other social activities. In early recovery however, the newly recovering person is often attracted to those who use drugs.

FIGURE 6.4. In abstinence-only recovery, the cessation of substances marks the beginning of the action stage.

The old saying "birds of a feather flock together" is quite applicable here. People in early addiction recovery are often attracted to people they are comfortable with. In early recovery, there usually hasn't been enough change to be attracted to the "squares" who haven't used substances. Often, they are attracted to people who use substances excessively but are not open about it, or to those who are code-pendent. This is where a 12-step program can again help, as the recovering person is able to meet people in the same situation: former substance users who want to remain substance free. But if one decides not to participate in a 12-step program, a good idea would be to develop some sober support from people the person in early recovery already has in her or his life. This may be the family (although often the family can be just as stressful as helpful to someone in early recovery), people one knows but who weren't formerly associated with, or members of a therapy group. A significant factor is to be cognizant of one's new friends. The friends one makes early in recovery often test one's resolve to remain abstinent.

The Beginning of Lasting Change

There is no clear-cut path of recovery that fits everyone. Some stop substances and then gain internal motivation, possibly while in inpatient treatment. Others change substances, try controlled use, or any variation of the preparation stage discussed above. Some people move up and back in the stages of change, entering the action stage, then returning to the preparation or contemplation stages. But once in the action stage, there are several things the recovering person and the counselor can do to foster more effective recovery.

One of the important things that has to occur is the gaining of understanding of how addiction may have occurred for that individual. This is vital, as it helps to begin removing the shame felt by the addicted person.

Often, when those who are caught in an addiction begin recovery, they believe that they are morally weak or crazy or otherwise fully to blame for their addiction. This belief is often embedded in his or her psyche, and despite attempts to rationalize and justify their substance use, underneath they feel different and possibly inferior to those who do not use. Early in the recovery process, it is essential to present varied theories on how individuals come to be addicted. There is no one-size-fits-all answer to who will develop an addiction. Addictions to substances or behaviors have many causes. No one theory is absolutely correct, and individuals will identify themselves as falling into several different categories. For example, a client may identify himself as having a disease (the disease concept), will also identify that he grew up in a home with an addicted parent (social learning theory), and will recognize that he experienced abuse and neglect (trauma theory). The theory of addictive personality could be attributed to any of these categories and may fall into any of the three. What is key is that the client identifies what he believes led to his addiction.

In teaching courses on the psychology of drugs, we sometimes give the assignment to students to identify their perception of how addiction originates and their perception of the addict. In hearing the students' views, we are often astounded that the perception of the addict is as a weak-minded, weak-willed, or immoral person who has not developed the ability to walk the line that society prescribes. Often, the view of a disease concept or genetic predisposition is thought of as an excuse for the addict to behave the way he or she wants. This is a perception we wish to challenge and which is undesirable if one is to be a therapist working with this population. Many people take the view that everyone should be held accountable for their decisions. As therapists, we agree. However, it must be understood that people often make their decisions as a result of unconscious factors or a physiological driving force.

Those who study and embrace psychology come to understand the power the unconscious wields over so much of our lives—so much of our thoughts and so much of our feelings. When you understand this, yet still believe people are accountable for their behavior, it is central to reconcile these two beliefs. To do this, an acceptance that unconsciousness and biological forces are undergirding factors is a prerequisite. From there, the therapist can help the client become more self-aware and identify unconscious processes. In doing so, respect for the power of their unconscious will naturally occur. Chapter 4 discussed some of the automatic (and often largely unconscious) thoughts that contribute to perpetuating an addiction. Throughout the stages of change, it is necessary to be cognizant of this and, when necessary, challenge thinking.

The Stages of Change Related to the Recovery Process

During the preparation stage (while trying out new behaviors) or at the beginning of the next stage (action), the recovering person may engage in 12-step meetings and his respective process of beginning to work the steps.

The action stage is a long stage encompassing the *true* beginning of recovery, where stabilization begins and continues for the first year. In this, the individual begins to stabilize, is abstinent, and begins to build sober support and identify cues to urges for substance use. This stage begins with the resolution of withdrawal symptoms. **Acute withdrawal** describes the short-term withdrawal from chemicals and includes symptoms such as tremors, sweating, elevated blood pressure, flu-like symptoms, and possibly seizures. When severe, these acute withdrawal symptoms require medical detoxification to reduce the risk of serious medical complications, including death. Drugs which require medical detoxification include opiates, benzodiazepines, alcohol, and sedatives.

Post-acute withdrawal (PAW) refers to the long-term effects of withdrawal, including depressed mood, difficulty in thinking clearly, managing feelings, memory problems, difficulty in sleeping restfully, and managing stress. Symptoms of PAW become more pronounced in times of stress. In other words, stress can trigger PAW. Managing PAW is pivotal to remaining abstinent. It is important to understand that PAW results from long-term drug use. Just knowing this is a normal response can be helpful. It is also imperative to learn to recognize the symptoms, accept them as part of the addiction, talk to others when they are experienced, keep active in recovery activities, eat well, avoid excessive caffeine and nicotine, use relaxation and meditation, sleep regularly, engage in exercise, and learn stress management techniques.

Most addicts in the beginning of their recovery report persistent cravings. As we mentioned in Chapter 4, Gorski describes the following as factors that contribute to addictive preoccupation that perpetuates cravings.

Euphoric recall: focusing on and exaggerating the good memories of use; also called rosy recollection

Positive expectancy: the belief that substance use will bring us pain-free pleasure, due to experiences in the early part of addiction

Trigger event: anything that causes sudden stress, pain, or discomfort

Obsession: inability to stop thinking about using; usually fostered by euphoric recall and positive expectancy

Compulsion: a feeling process that occurs in the gut; a strong, irrational desire to do something that is not in the person's best interest

Craving: a body or tissue hunger for substances

FIGURE 6.5. Counseling during the action stage often focuses on identifying triggers and new coping strategies.

In this stage, then, it is important for the client to identify triggers to thoughts of using. Once triggered, it is chief to recognize when the individual is having euphoric recall and is toying with positive expectancy. One way to combat this is by "playing the whole tape." This refers to thinking about the incident to its true conclusion and consequences. Although there were good times when using substances, it is beneficial to ask, "What was the end result?" At the very least, it would seem that treatment became necessary. Rarely does someone enter treatment without having experienced negative consequences. So, when experiencing these early addictive preoccupation contributors, it is imperative to challenge these thoughts, as demonstrated in Chapter 4.

Also in early recovery—especially true in the first attempt—a common stage is the **honeymoon stage**, or as it is called in AA, the **pink cloud**. In this phenomenon, the individual feels great about recovery, about life, about the changes they are making. This is a double-edged sword. Of course, it feels great and also allows the individual to get some distance between him and his last use. On the other side of the coin, this feeling is often mistaken for a newfound way of being. This can also lead to a huge letdown. Often in AA they say, "When you are on a pink cloud, you will need a pink parachute."

In group therapy, individuals may experience the "honeymoon" stage of recovery. When people are in this stage, it can be more difficult to work on issues because they feel so good, and it seems nothing affects them much. In one particular group, the therapist focused the topic on what types of things the members could do to maintain or get back to this serene feeling they were experiencing. Some members embraced the topic and identified things such as working out, reading and meditating, and other positive behaviors. One member, however, reported that this was his new self and that it was just how he was going to be now that he ceased substances. Unfortunately, he was in for a big letdown a few months later, but eventually he was able to laugh about his statement. This example illuminates several things: First, it is sometimes difficult to work with clients in this stage because they actually believe they might remain with this newfound state of mind forever. Second, it is important for clients to be prepared for an ending of this honeymoon stage; and third, it is important to meet them in their state of mind and not be condescending or too confrontational, causing a rupture in the therapeutic relationship.

Evidently, the process of addiction is not just a problem with substances; it is the dysfunctional way in which an individual thinks that perpetuates the addiction. One of the first tasks in the recovery process is to gain understanding of the disease of addiction. It is essential to recognize that each addict has a part of his thinking process devoted to maintaining addiction and/or promoting self-indulgent behaviors. This other side of his thinking has been referred to in several ways: addictive thinking, the beast, the little dope fiend on my shoulder, or simply the addictive self. Understanding that this dysfunctional thinking process exists and recognizing its thoughts is a big part of understanding addiction. In addition, it is beneficial to identify the behaviors and personality traits that belong to the addicted self as separate and opposed to the individual's true self. Many professionals recommend the following:

1. Have the client write an abbreviated version of his life story starting in childhood.
2. Have him summarize the major events in his life by using a timeline.
3. Create a timeline that outlines his drug and alcohol history and its progression.
4. Compare the two timelines, noting major life events and substance-use patterns. (It often happens that substance users will not see the parallels between major events in their lives and the beginning or substantial increases of substance use until they complete this assignment or have otherwise accomplished this in talk therapy.)

It is frequently said in psychology that for every behavior there is a reward. This is also true of substance use. Another recommended exercise illuminates some reasons drugs and alcohol might have been used. It consists of discussing the strengths one had when using and what type of situations were avoided through the use of substances. Of course, it will be important to find out how to develop those strengths in recovery, or accept the weaknesses and develop new coping mechanisms for the situations that led to substance use. It is beneficial to ask the client the following:

1. What strengths were gained from substance use?
2. What weaknesses were compensated for?
3. What situations were avoided through substance use?

In addiction recovery, it is often imperative for clients to accept that addiction is a journey they will travel throughout their lives. This idea is so prevalent in psychology, it is called the **recovery model**. Although it began in the treatment of alcoholism, the model is now being applied to schizophrenia and other psychotic disorders, as well as post-traumatic stress disorder (PTSD). Resilience, control over problems, and gaining control over life is the focus of the recovery model (Jacob, 2015). In the article "Applying Recovery Principles to the Treatment of Trauma," Smith and colleagues discuss how to apply nine recovery principles. The principles are as follows:

(1) being supported by others, including the important role of community and social support; (2) renewing hope and commitment through spirituality or other means; (3) engaging in meaningful activities through reclaiming social roles held prior to illness onset and/or identifying new ones; (4) redefining oneself by shifting the view of mental illness to include an understanding that it is only one aspect of the self, rather than all encompassing; (5) incorporating illness by accepting any limits that may persist due to mental illness; (6) overcoming stigma related to having a mental illness; (7) assuming control over treatment and choices; (8) managing symptoms; and (9) becoming empowered and exercising citizenship. (Smith, Hyman, Andres-Hyman, Ruiz, & Davidson, 2016)

The principle of accepting limits includes accepting one has a disorder that affects thinking and will last the rest of one's life. This acceptance needs to occur on both a cognitive and emotional level. The previous paragraphs address the cognitive level. To accept the addiction—and all it has wrought in life—one must also deal with the emotions that were ignored due to substance use. When discussing these emotions in early recovery, many people feel shame and guilt. These feelings need to be resolved in order to completely accept addiction. Part of the acceptance of addiction is working toward the resolution of the pain of the addiction experience.

Some common emotional pitfalls one might experience in this stage are as follows:

- minimizing addiction
- shame and guilt
- not dealing with traumatic or other unresolved feelings from the past

- overconfidence
- not prioritizing recovery and personal growth
- **the wall** (the newness of recovery wears off and the realization that there is much more work to be done).

Typical addiction treatment practically demands the dual treatment of individual/group therapy and a 12-step self-help support group. There are specific gains achieved by attending a 12-step group that simply cannot be attained through individual treatment. Some of the 12-step benefits that can help with these goals are as follows:

- Hearing others' stories at meetings: There is a richness in exposure to diverse circumstances and contexts of addiction that can only be heard once within a group.
- Speaking at meetings: Testimony to one's pain, struggle, and anguish before a group of like-minded individuals provides an incredible sense of strength and support.
- Getting a sponsor: Being mentored, guided, and supported by someone who has successfully moved through the steps is inspirational to a newly recovering addict.

Relating to what others have done as a result of their addiction fosters self-forgiveness. A 12-step program is a forum for dealing with emotions.

The 12-steps of recovery can take anywhere from a few months to a year or more to complete. The significant thing is to focus on the recovery. Often, once stability occurs, the individual too quickly returns to regular daily activity (this is not to say people in early recovery shouldn't work or take care of whatever responsibilities they have). However, often their focus on recovery wanes as normal activity becomes the priority. The suggestion is that recovery remains the largest priority. There is nearly always a lot of work to be done in the first year of recovery. Building sober support, developing new activities, discovering trigger events, challenging irrational thinking, focusing on rebuilding relationships—all are important tasks for the person beginning in recovery. And although life responsibilities may have been neglected during substance use, putting recovery efforts on the back burner can contribute to relapse.

The next stage of change according to Prochaska, Norcross, and DiClemente is the maintenance stage. During this stage, which begins in middle recovery and lasts through late recovery, continued efforts are made toward self-improvement.

Middle recovery begins the return to lifestyle balance. During this stage, the struggle to remain abstinent has subsided. The focus can now shift to other areas of importance, including relationships, employment advancement, ongoing health, working on emotions, and controlling of behavior. There is an acceptance of responsibility for behavior; thinking continues to clear, and the capability for true honesty grows. New coping mechanisms are developed as well as new skills for dealing with feelings and situations. There is an increasing responsibility for thinking and behavior as well as for the recovery program. This brings increasing control in the recovering individual's life along with an awareness of empowerment. During this stage, there is an increasing ability to handle life's ups and downs, which have become less frequent due to the practicing of good judgment. It is also common to see a slight decrease in 12-step program attendance to meet other needs, which will help facilitate a balanced lifestyle. The importance of a healthy diet, avoiding nicotine and excessive amounts of caffeine, and regular exercise bears repeating.

Some pitfalls common to the middle stage of recovery include complacency, fear, and **unnecessary** stress caused by improper diet (too much caffeine and nicotine are common offenders here).

The goal of traditional addiction recovery is not just abstinence but spiritual awakening. The late stage of recovery, for those who venture into it, is about self-actualization, spiritual awakening, enlightenment, or any other name you might choose to call it. In an excellent book that draws parallels between Maslow's hierarchy of needs and the 12-step program, *The Hierarchy of Recovery: From Abstinence to Self-Actualization*, Robert Helgoe describes the push-and-pull phase of recovery. In the push phase, the recovering individual is brought into recovery by consequences. The individual remains in recovery at this stage to avoid the return of consequences. As recovery is maintained, Helgoe describes an individual moving into the pull phase of recovery. In this stage, it is no longer the fear of consequences that continues sobriety, but instead a desire to self-actualize, to be all one can be. This is the second tier of addiction treatment. Those in recovery may stay in therapy or return to it, may work in a structured self-help group (such as 12-step groups or other support groups), or otherwise seek help with living purposefully and finding meaning in life, as well as working to recognize their potential. A humanistic approach is often of the best use in this tier.

This **self-actualization** process can come about in many ways, including through vigorous 12-step work, through therapy, or through spiritual or religious means. There is no one path to actualization or enlightenment, so the person in recovery must look at the paths of others and decide his own.

The Grieving Process in Addiction Recovery

This section will address the importance of the **grieving process** to sustaining addiction recovery. In order to accomplish this, we utilize several sources that discuss the grieving process, including Elisabeth Kübler-Ross's stages of grieving, J. William Worden's book *Grief Counseling and Grief Therapy*, and Robert Helgoe's book *The Hierarchy of Recovery*. As usual, some of our experiences will also be included.

There are three reasons that the grieving process is central to sustained, rewarding recovery. The first is that many addicts have unresolved grief issues from their past. Perhaps the death of a relative or the dissolution of a close personal relationship has occurred. The use of drugs and

FIGURE 6.6. Grieving is an integral stage in the recovery process. Not only does the individual have to deal with any delayed grief from what was lost in addiction, but the individual must grieve the loss of the addiction itself.

alcohol hampers the grieving process, resulting in a **delayed grief** reaction. The loss is not grieved until the addictive use of drugs and alcohol is ceased and the feelings surrounding the loss are felt and processed.

For many in addiction recovery, this requires a focus on the loss in therapy. Many who enter inpatient facilities have this opportunity and discuss unresolved grief issues in group therapy. Those who enter outpatient therapy, however, do not generally have daily groups to discuss issues. As a result, daily events and trials and tribulations may inhibit grief issues that need to be resolved from surfacing.

A second reason that grieving is significant to recovery is due to the losses that occur because of addictive use. Many recovering addicts grieve over time they have lost with family, time lost in or starting their careers, and missed opportunities. Recovering addicts compare their progress in their lives to that of nonaddicted peers, and they appear to fall short. Their peers have moved on in their careers, have had and raised families, and have many amenities that a person new to recovery may lack. This issue is quite common and is important to address in addiction recovery treatment.

One solution is to focus on the subjects of clients' comparisons. As therapists, we have asked clients when they compare themselves to nonaddicted peers, "Where were you six months ago? How has your life changed since then? Is it really logical to compare yourself to someone who didn't have the issues you had?" This puts the focus back on the progress—sometimes the enormous progress—a client has made rather than allowing him to focus on the negative aspects of what he didn't accomplish in the years he was using substances.

In order to discuss the third reason that the grieving process is essential to rewarding recovery, it is necessary to return to a theory from Helgoe's book,

The Hierarchy of Recovery. As described above, Helgoe (2002) divides recovery into two phases, the first one being the **push phase**, which in this case is toward the crisis or events which led to treatment. More concisely, the recovering addicts are staying clean to avoid the consequences they experienced due to active addiction. Their motivation is largely to avoid the life they were living, being pushed from an old life to a new.

In the **pull phase**, the recovering persons are drawn toward a more spiritual and fulfilling life. The focus of recovery is no longer avoidance of the old way of living but attraction to a new way of being and enjoyment of the rewards of recovery in the present. Furthermore, focus on continued self-discovery, and eventually self-expression, is the focus.

Helgoe believes that in order to move into the pull phase of recovery, where the rewards of recovery are found, a person must complete the grieving process for his or her addiction. Facing the fact that the use of a substance such as alcohol or drugs can never be relied upon again is a painful experience for any addict. The reality of living the rest of your life without drugs and/or alcohol is sometimes nearly impossible to fathom. When addicts give up substances, they are giving up a friend, a lover, and possibly the only relief they know. True acceptance of powerlessness over substances is a true loss. Moreover, according to Kübler-Ross (2005), an authority on grief and grieving, we experience grief whenever we lose anything of importance.

As identified by Kübler-Ross (2005), there are five stages of grieving. They are as follows:

Denial: A belief that the news cannot be correct, due to the pain associated with the loss. This is in response to shock and the loss being too overwhelming.

FIGURE 6.7. Anger is an accepted stage of the grieving process. One may be angry at oneself, God, or life, or project anger onto others.

Anger: This intense emotion diminishes the experience of the pain that comes with the loss. The anger can be directed at a person or thing lost, at God, or at the self.

Bargaining: Hope leads to bargaining, a defense mechanism that delays the pain of the loss temporarily, until the hope is extinguished.

Depression: This deep state of sadness works to dull the pain of the loss because it dulls nearly all experience, internal and external (Helgoe, 2002, pp. 56–59). In addition, according to Helgoe (2002), "at this point people go in one of two directions: they either continue defending against the pain or they drop their defenses and experience the pain." If they choose to continue to defend against the pain and not experience it, they "may resort to previously used defenses (denial, anger, bargaining) and enter into what can be termed extended or chronic grief, a life-debilitating situation often misdiagnosed" (pp. 59–60).

Acceptance: The acceptance of the pain associated with the loss.

In the book *Grief Counseling and Grief Therapy* by J. William Worden (1991), the grief process is divided into four tasks. Worden describes the continued process after the individual has reached the stage of acceptance. In some regard, Worden's approach is a revisit of Kübler-Ross's stages, but putting actions to the stages, making them less passive. They are described as the following:

Task I—Accept the reality of the loss.
During this phase, the denial of the loss, including denial regarding the meaning of the loss and/or the irreversibility of the loss, is resolved. *Relates to shock, denial, and bargaining.*

Task II—Working through the pain.
During this phase the grieving work in relation to the pain is processed and resolved. Avoiding the pain prolongs the process, as does avoiding the anger. People avoid anger due to feeling guilty, such as being angry at the deceased or at God. In relation to addiction, recovering addicts may be angry at their loved ones for dying, angry with God for making them an addict, angry with the disease of addiction, angry at themselves for being addicts, and angry at those who can drink or use socially. They may have pain related to not being able to use again, and the acceptance of powerlessness may hurt their images of self-worth. *Relates to anger and depression.*

This is common in addiction and often is necessary to address in therapy. There have been countless cases in which clients have discussed their anger at others for being able to use or at themselves for not being able to use "normally." This can lead to shame and is therefore essential to address.

In the circumstance of someone grieving a lost loved one, this stage is exemplified when the bereaved remembers the deceased in a consistently positive light, feeling joy and positive nostalgia, rather than the sense of loss. Perhaps activities that were avoided because of remembrance of the deceased are begun again, and the emotional energy transforms from sadness to a more positive emotion.

In the situation where the addiction was grieved and accepted, emotional energy is transformed into a positive. The recovering person no longer resents those who can use and may now be able to return to activities that were avoided. New activities are embraced.

In one example, Brett, a 35-year-old Asian American male, had sustained recovery for over five years. He was in treatment focusing on issues of continued growth. When initially in treatment, and for at least the first year of recovery, Brett resented those who could use substances successfully. He would often speak in groups about the resentment that he couldn't use. By the time he returned to therapy, through his work in 12-step meetings and through reading, this had changed. He had developed new, more creative activities, such as writing a blog and working on a book. He no longer resented those who could use and instead accepted that he couldn't and strove for continued personal growth.

Task III—Adjustment to the environment.

During this phase, the individual may need to reidentify himself and take on new roles. *Relates to the beginning of acceptance.*

Task IV—Emotional relocation of the loss.

The emotional energy once tied to the loss is transferred and converted into positive emotions. This is the final task, and as it relates to recovery, the individual has now accepted the loss. This would lend itself to entering the pull stage of recovery, as identified by Helgoe (2002). *Relates to the acceptance stage.*

There is an array of feelings that are considered normal in the grieving process. These include, but are not limited to, sadness, anger, guilt and self-reproach, anxiety, loneliness, fatigue, helplessness, shock, yearning, emancipation, relief, and numbness.

There are several complications that can occur during the grieving process. These include the following:

Delayed grief: the immediate emotional response is insufficient to the loss (grief counseling and grief therapy)

Extended grief: emotional flatness, feelings of guilt

Chronic grief: the continued use of defenses and not dealing with the pain associated with grief results in this (*Hierarchy of Recovery,* p. 65)

It is vital to be aware of the client's grieving process in relation to substances and to assist him in moving through any of the areas of grief he may be experiencing. In some cases, 12-step meetings can be helpful as members relate to one another's grieving processes.

Summary

The process of recovery is, by any standard, a long and complicated process. Researchers (Prochaska, Norcross, and DiClemente; Gorski) and writers (Helgoe, Gorski) have focused on this process and attempted to identify stages that are common to most in addiction recovery.

Prochaska, Norcross, and DiClemente's stages of change help the clinician recognize the stage of change the client is in, so as to match his interventions to the client's state. This fosters both a more understanding approach toward the client as well as more realistic expectations of his abilities, and thereby an increased chance of success for the client.

The stages of recovery are extremely helpful in illuminating what the recovering individual can expect and can help to normalize what he is experiencing. Individuals and therapists alike can utilize these signs to ascertain what stage the recovering individual is in and what some of the pitfalls might be. Additionally, these stages provide guidance and hope toward a more stable future in recovery.

Grief is an often-misunderstood and significant dynamic in the recovery process. Those entering recovery will grieve the loss of their substance or addictive behavior. They may also have complicated grief responses to other losses while actively using or as a result of their addiction. Understanding these processes are integral to a healthy recovery process.

Key Terms

Precontemplation	Maintenance	Marijuana maintenance
Contemplation	Trigger	Acute withdrawal
Preparation	Self-help support groups	Post-acute withdrawal
Action stage		Euphoric recall

Positive expectancy

Trigger event

Obsession

Compulsion

Craving

Honeymoon stage

Pink cloud

Recovery model

The wall

Middle recovery

Self-actualization

Grieving process

Delayed grief

Push phase

Pull phase

Extended grief

Chronic grief

Coping mechanism

CHAPTER SEVEN

Fighting Temptation

Learning Objectives

- Explain what the authors mean by old brain behavior.
- Differentiate between a thought, urge, and craving, and discuss how they relate to the recovery process.
- Describe interventions for each level of desire.
- Explain some of the circumstances under which a temptation might occur.
- Identify what leads to increased levels of desire.
- Discuss how increases in levels of temptation can be interrupted.

Introduction

One of the reasons it is imperative for recovering addicts to have supportive people in their lives (beyond the obvious fact that support just makes life easier in general) is to fight temptation; fighting temptation can be extremely difficult in early recovery. It is a commonly mentioned statistic that out of 10 people who seek treatment for addiction, only one remains abstinent successfully for the long term. First, seeking treatment needs to be defined. It is simply the act of presenting for an evaluation. It does not denote actually entering treatment or following up on a referral. Next, "successfully" needs to be defined. Some treatment professionals view success as complete abstinence maintained for life. This is a very strict definition and often the expectation of those treating addiction. Although it is a strict and perfectionistic goal, it is also the safest goal. If an addiction professional were to tell someone entering recovery that a few relapses are inevitable, it runs the risk of the client interpreting this to mean he or she *will* relapse. Imagine, considering what you know about how addiction distorts thinking, that the newly recovering person hears, "Well, we expect a few relapses, and that's okay." We've heard addicts entering recovery say that because the odds of recovery are so bad they should just go out and use now! As such, it is difficult to determine what the absolute correct path to take with a client is. The complete abstinence model reeks of perfection and unrealistic expectations, and the alternative of emphasizing that eventual relapses are acceptable seems to set the client up for distorted thinking. The best approach is one of balance and, of course, individualized treatment.

One must keep in mind that it is truly a struggle to fight the temptation to use a substance when one has an addiction. For example, let's look at the temptation involved in dieting. Most people can relate to this. Think of a time, even if it was for blood work or a medical procedure, when you were not allowed to eat for a period of time. You were hungry, there may have been food easily accessible, and yet you had to be disciplined and not eat because the consequences of ruining the procedure or tainting the results of your blood work outweighed the pleasure of giving in. It is very likely the individual will be successful when it is for one day. However, say you decided to begin a diet that requires you to complete your last meal at 5:00 p.m., which means you can't eat for at least another 14 hours (breakfast). The expectation is you do this day in and day out. There is an increased possibility you will give in. Temptation, whatever its form, is difficult to fight.

When this is coupled with withdrawal symptoms, whether they are acute or post-acute (as discussed in Chapter 6), temptation to use a substance is even harder to fight. The individual is experiencing difficult biological and psychological phenomena that can easily be remedied by the use of his substance of choice. Although there may be viable reasons not to use a substance, if the temptation is great and when left unchallenged, thinking becomes distorted and a slip or relapse becomes more likely.

Old Brain Behavior

Another perspective of substance craving is seeing it as **old brain behavior**. The old brain, the part of the brain we share with all animals, is driven by instinct. This is where hunger, thirst, and sexual desire all originate. This part of the brain is one of the areas affected by repeated substance use. Once an addiction has developed, it is this part of the brain that produces craving. When an addict goes without drugs or alcohol for a period, it resembles going without food, drink, or sex for a period. Imagine yourself thirsty, having had no water or other liquids for a day. Wouldn't drinking take priority over almost every other conceivable responsibility? For an addict, using a substance feels like it is about survival.

> Janet is a 43-year-old Native American female. She is divorced with two children, aged 20 and 22. Since her divorce two years ago and her children moving out, Janet has fallen into a depression that she copes with through alcohol. Initially, Janet began drinking in the evenings to help fill the silence and numb the pain of being alone. As she developed tolerance, she discovered that she could experience a pervasive sense of relief if she drank sporadically throughout the day instead of at night only. Janet felt she had discovered a way to manage the "ache." She no longer experienced emptiness or pain because of her "clever" strategy. In addition, she was still able to go to work and function as usual—or so she thought. Janet's coworkers noticed a significant change in her behavior. She wasn't completing tasks on time, and she had a noticeable odor of alcohol throughout the day. After two months, Janet was faced with an intervention. As each person explained to her that her behavior was destructive, Janet resisted. According to Janet, "This is who I am. I need alcohol like I need food. You take this away from me and I will die." This distorted thinking is a direct reflection of Janet's old brain behavior. The threat of taking away her alcohol increasingly angered her to the point where she walked out of the intervention, stopped speaking to her family, and quit her job.

As expressed in Chapter 4, thinking becomes distorted when one has an addiction. Rationalizing substance use, minimizing the consequences or their severity, or any of the other cognitive distortions may play a part in the addict's initiation of substance use or inability to stop when things start to go wrong. It is essential to remember that distortions in thinking are prevalent in addiction. Coupled with these cognitive distortions is the strong physical yearning people experience for the substance. This physical yearning can be so powerful that it controls the person's life and clouds the lens of perception.

Levels of Desire

There are three levels of desire for substance use. The first level of desire, which is the easiest to effect change, is a thought. This is simply an idea that a substance would be able to provide relief from or enhance an experience.

Thoughts of substance use are common. Anyone who has had an addiction will tell you that thoughts of use occur. For an addict in recovery, this is especially dangerous. It has been estimated that the average human has between 12,000 and 70,000 thoughts a day. Even if you go with the lower number, that is a great many thoughts. Someone who is in early recovery from addiction may think of substance use a hundred times a day.

Of course, all thoughts are not necessarily fully conscious, and for our purposes we are focusing only on conscious thoughts. When someone in recovery recognizes he is thinking of substance use, there are a couple courses of action. First, and most opportune, is when the individual challenges the thought. As discussed in Chapter 4, the thoughts underlying and contributing to the idea of substance use can be weighed and evaluated to determine if it is a distortion of thinking. In fact, if someone accepts he has an addiction and is unlikely to control substance use, any thought of use is a cognitive distortion, or just simply irrational. Often when a thought of substance use is recognized, it can simply be dismissed as absurd. This becomes easier with time away from the substance. Unfortunately, many people, those with addiction issues included, do not make logical decisions.

One problem in our culture is we give thoughts too much merit. Too many people take their thoughts as more meaningful than they are. As therapists, we've seen the effects of taking thoughts too seriously. A person may admonish herself for her thoughts, leading to feelings of shame, guilt, or depression. Others experience a great deal of anxiety as a result of their thoughts and providing thoughts with too much merit. For those with addictions, a slip or relapse begins as a result of their thoughts. One would be better off to heed the advice of Dan Millman's character Socrates in the movie *Peaceful Warrior*: "The mind is just a reflex organ. It reacts to everything. Fills your head with millions of random thoughts a day. None of those thoughts reveal any more about you than a freckle does at the end of your nose."

One way to decrease the power of a thought to use is simply by discussing it. This is one of the benefits of sober support, discussed in Chapter 5. Often someone who understands addiction will relate to the thought, normalize it, and help challenge it. One problem is people are often too ashamed or embarrassed to share their thoughts. Another is that often people in early recovery don't have others around them for support who have been through the struggles with temptation. This can be remedied through 12-step meetings, as discussed in Chapter 5. However, many who enter recovery do not want to attend meetings.

A second course of action some in recovery take in regard to thoughts of substance use is to **entertain the thought**. This is when the person now takes control of the automatic thought and plays with it. He or she might think of how nice it would be to use, or how good it would feel. He might visualize using the substance, where he would obtain it, or in what situation he could get away with it. He might plan it out, while never meaning to follow through. He may just view this as daydreaming, and believe it harmless fantasy. Sometimes addicts get a rush talking about their life of drug use. They may be telling a story and then relish in the idea of it. However, unchecked and unchallenged, thoughts lead to urges.

An **urge**, the second level of desire, can best be described as a motivation for substance use. It is stronger than a thought, but can still be challenged. At the point a thought becomes an urge, it has gained momentum. Sometimes this is a result of having entertained the thought. Sometimes it can be the result of stress and other negative feelings that create more regular and powerful escapist thoughts (which, for a substance user, often revolve around getting high). One way to describe an urge is as recurrent and stronger thoughts that at times will not relent. Although the thought is now gaining momentum, it can be reversed by again thinking through the consequences or talking about the urge with a person supportive of sobriety, or through distraction with a more appropriate activity. Sometimes more than one strategy is necessary. When an urge is at its worst, the individual would benefit from continuing trying different strategies to combat it. But if the urge continues, it may become a craving.

A **craving**, the third level of desire, is described as a bodily hunger for something. At this point, it becomes extremely uncomfortable for the addict not to use. This isn't just a result of the physical-chemical addiction the body may have. It is true that when someone is addicted to a drug (like opioids, alcohol, benzodiazepines, and other sedatives, as well as nicotine and even cannabis), it may likely cause a physical dependence that will perpetuate the need for continued use to achieve relief or a greater desired effect. However, cravings can also occur as a result of environmental and psychological triggers long after the substance is ceased. This can occur, as already discussed, when thoughts and urges go unchecked and, worse, when they are entertained. In Chapter 6, rosy recollection and euphoric recall were discussed. These thought patterns help perpetuate the entertainment of the drug use thought. Without interruption, this can result in a craving.

Cravings early in recovery are the strongest when a recovering person is feeling overwhelmed by life's stressors, when experiencing strong negative emotions, or when experiencing periods of self-deprecation. One strategy that works in these times is a strong belief in the first step of the 12-step program: that the individual is powerless over addiction and that life had been unmanageable as a result. When an individual knows that substance use would again turn his life into the hell it had been previously, he is able to use this belief to challenge the temptation. A therapist can discuss with a client the times over the course of his substance use he had tried to temper use or to use successfully and elicit how none of these attempts had worked. Many substance users have tried changing the substance to a "lighter" drug (e.g., using alcohol or marijuana instead of cocaine or heroin), changing what they drank (from liquor to beer or wine), trying to limit use to evening hours or certain days of the week, trying to start using later in the day, trying to nurse a drink, trying to only use on weekends, and even asking friends to keep them from using too much. For many with addictions, none of these attempts had worked, and he or she had always returned to the addicted use of substances—and all of the consequences that came with it. This accumulation of events is the essence of Step 1. (A reminder: Step 1, We admitted we were powerless, and that our lives had become unmanageable). The addict's thinking, having cleared as a result of early recovery, may allow him to see that no matter what he had tried during the course of addiction, a return to addictive substance use followed. This would indicate a level of powerlessness, like the first step purports.

The importance of accepting one's inability to control the substance cannot be overemphasized. Thoughts that originate in addictive thinking convince the newly recovering person that he might be able to use one more time or control it this time. Step 1 is the only step necessary to remain abstinent. The other steps are geared toward making one's sobriety happier. Accepting that the use of a substance will return the addicted user to his previous level of use, despite what his addictive thinking might be telling him, is often essential for many to maintain abstinence. It is also an effective cognitive challenge. As stated above, if I am powerless and cannot control my substance use, it is irrational to even think of using.

A more difficult craving to challenge is one that arises as a result of overwhelming negative emotions. Not everyone relapses as a result of cognitive distortions. Often people make decisions they know are poor, based on emotional desires. This is also true of relapse into substance use. Often someone experiencing a craving as a result of difficult emotions will know that substance use will be detrimental. He won't be convincing himself he can control it or that it'll be only a one-time use. Instead, his feelings are so averse, he just doesn't care what will happen. He just wants to escape.

In this case, sober support and working through the feelings are generally the best course. The individual would need to be willing to talk, which is often an obstacle. In AA, they sometimes discuss "the phone weighing a ton." This, of course, is a metaphor for not wanting to ask for help. In cases of strong urges, an individual would benefit from staying around those who are supportive, and thereby not having as much opportunity to act on the craving.

Addictive thinking cannot be underestimated, and it remains an issue throughout recovery. Working in the field of addiction treatment, a therapist will inevitably encounter many incidents of it. Although it is usually most common in early recovery, sometimes, even after years of

FIGURE 7.1. Support is an integral part of the recovery model. It is imperative to develop relationships supportive of recovery.

sobriety a recovering person might become convinced that perhaps overindulgence in substance use was just part of the tumultuous teenage (and early adulthood) years. Thoughts that it was probably just rebellious youth might occur, and now that one is older, perhaps he or she really isn't an addict, and it isn't necessary to continue to remain abstinent. The idea of controlled use seems logical and worth a try. For a select few people, it is possible. This topic will be addressed in the chapter on harm reduction. But for the majority, it is simply addictive thinking and will lead to further, and often worse, problems. For discussion here, we are focusing on the safest therapeutic mindset, one of complete abstinence.

The example above demonstrates a couple of things: First, addictive thinking has the ability to create thoughts, urges, and cravings, and never completely subsides. A person in recovery is always at risk of his thinking leading to a return to substance use. Second, addictive thinking is, as Narcotics Anonymous maintains, "**cunning, baffling, and powerful.**" The addicted mind can trick an individual into believing substance use is a viable option, when in truth it leads to further destruction. Third, some sort of program of personal growth is essential to challenging and overcoming the addiction. If the recovering individual is able to utilize some of the techniques discussed earlier for evaluating the rationality of thoughts, she can determine that thoughts of substance use are distorted. She can then use the evidence she has accumulated, both in her addiction and in recovery, to make a more rational decision: generally, continued abstinence. It is vital, however, for the client to understand that temptation is normal and that thoughts of use will lose their frequency and intensity as abstinence progresses, but that one is always at risk of slipping into old patterns of thinking. It is also essential to understand that for many, strong negative feelings can contribute to temptation, and one would benefit from learning to cope with and handle them more appropriately.

Dean had been in recovery for about three months. It was his first time in recovery, and he had been on a pink cloud. He had barely had any thoughts of using, let alone an urge or craving. He wondered what everyone in the treatment center had been worried about; recovery was much easier than anyone seemed to anticipate. He had been relishing his new life.

But today was different. For the first time since getting out of rehab, the stress of work seemed to be getting to him. He was looking forward to meeting his girlfriend for dinner and a movie later. Work was particularly mundane today. He realized he had a passing thought of getting a beer during lunch with some coworkers, as he had done many times in the past. He was a little shocked by the thought, but dismissed it easily without mention. About an hour later, he got a text from his girlfriend. She needed to cancel the date because she had forgotten about previous plans with her sister. Dean was disappointed. He had been looking forward to it and used the plans with her as something to look forward to while having a particularly long day at work. Again, a thought of having a beer, this time after work, popped in his head. This time, rather than dismissing it as ridiculous, he toyed with the idea. He remembered how much fun it had been in the past to laugh and joke with his peers while having a few beers. He remembered how good beer tasted and how it was the perfect complement to the local pub's grilled shrimp and onion rings. As he thought about it, he realized how much he missed hanging out with the guys on a Friday night after work. And to boot, there was a playoff game tonight, making everything more exciting and fun.

Dean shook off the thought temporarily, but the workday grew more stressful. Without his date to look forward to, the thought of going home to his apartment felt like punishment. Work felt like punishment. All he could think about was how good it would be to have a beer and hang out with the guys. His thoughts became an urge; he now wanted a beer or two. He started thinking how he could handle a few beers; after all, look how well he's done. He had a brief thought of calling his sponsor or outpatient therapist, but it was fleeting and he didn't want to bother either of them. He had been so strong for so long, he didn't want to appear weak.

As he piled on the negativity of the day, the urge grew stronger. By the end of the day, he felt like he needed a beer. In fact, that was the predominant contemplation in his head: "I need a drink. One or two can't hurt."

Building Resilience

Resilience is defined for our purposes as one's ability to bend (not break) in the face of stress and to return to one's previous level of functioning. Resilience and **willpower** have a lot in common, and increasing one positively impacts the other. Before we discuss that, a point needs to be made about willpower and addiction.

For a very long time, addiction was seen as a lack of willpower. This was synonymous with the theory of moral weakness, which is described as the first wave of addiction treatment. People who developed addiction were seen as weak minded. Many of you reading this may see that as an outdated concept. And although it is, many still have that mindset. Students in these classes have shared variations of this theory when discussing personal theories regarding how someone develops an addiction. Your authors are not advocates of the moral weakness theory, and our focus here on building resilience should not be mistaken for suggesting addicts are weak generally. The fact is that everyone can benefit from enhancing their self-control and understanding factors that increase their resiliency.

Resiliency, adapting to and withstanding stress and continuing successfully despite adversity, is considered a process by Emmy Werner, a researcher in the area of resilience (Werner & Brendtro, 2012). Resiliency can be learned, and people get better at being more resilient.

Resiliency requires a level of willpower. Both resiliency and willpower are perceived as limited resources. This means both can be depleted through overuse. Conversely, positively influencing one will increase the other. Research indicates willpower is influenced by perception (Job, Walton, Bernecker, & Dweck, 2013). Therefore, helping the recovering person alter their perception of adverse circumstances can increase resilience. This returns us to the topic of acceptance and mindfulness, discussed in Chapter 4. Utilizing mindfulness and acceptance alters perception of a situation, and thereby builds resilience. Generally, if one is able to cease the stories he says about a difficult situation, about it not being fair, about it being too difficult, about it being so horrible, and face it more objectively and presently, it becomes less overwhelming. A good example of this comes from the 12-step program's idea of "one day at a time." When one first learns the recovery suggestion of abstinence for the rest of one's life, this seems daunting if not impossible. However, the 12-step program suggests he only need be sober for the day, for the 24-hour period, which makes it more manageable. Before he knows it, the recovering person has been abstinent weeks, months, even years.

Research also indicates that one's perception of herself affects self-control. In an experiment focused on beliefs about self-control, partners who were told they scored high in self-control (the results were arbitrary) demonstrated more self-control when faced with the questions regarding their desire to contact an attractive potential partner (Hamburg & Pronk, 2015). In other words, their belief that they had high self-control led to more self-control. It is even suggested that one can increase their chance of successfully completing tasks through changing their self-talk. Those who adapt the belief that they are that type of person rather than simply changing a behavior (e.g., believing you are a nonsmoker rather than believing you are quitting smoking) are more successful. So, the person who identifies as someone who doesn't do drugs may have more success than the one who is "trying to quit." This reinforces the idea of how important self-talk is. Your authors have encountered many in treatment who self-identify as "chronic relapsers." An important aspect of early sessions is to change this self-image and self-talk.

The main focus of Chapter 4 is how self-deceived someone beginning recovery from an addiction can be. The use of mindfulness and questioning thinking can be of assistance. The ability to step back from thinking and view one's thoughts objectively can be an asset in building resilience and willpower. Additionally, as discussed in his book *Conquest of Mind* (2010), Eknath Easwaran describes the mind as a spoiled child and suggests treating it as you would any two-year-old. If the recovering person can view his mind this way, the decision can be made not to give in to its every desire, as you wouldn't a child. This mindset leads to more willpower and increased self-control. Every moment is an opportunity to be empowered.

Summary

Temptation, whatever its source, is powerful. Most people can relate to giving in to temptation in some way. Temptation toward returning to substance use is no different and is likely even more powerful, considering the way drugs affect the brain.

When discussing temptation in regard to addiction, there are three levels of desire: thoughts, urges, and craving. An example of a thought would be "it would be nice to have a beer right now." An urge is more intense, and denotes wanting: "Man, I'd really like a beer right now!" A craving is a bodily need: "Damn, I need a beer, I can't take this anymore!" As can be imagined, each becomes increasingly difficult to challenge and overcome. Using sober support and talking about thoughts and feelings, accepting that one has proof that their substance use cannot be controlled, understanding how addiction affects thinking, and determining that substances are not an option are ways in which one can successfully fight temptation. There will be further discussion of relapse prevention in Chapter 9.

Key Terms

Old brain behavior	Craving	Resilience
Entertain the thought	Cunning, baffling, and powerful	Willpower
Urge		

CHAPTER EIGHT

Gorski's Relapse Process

Learning Objectives

- Identify who Terence Gorski is and why his work is important.
- Explain the importance of understanding the relapse process.
- Discuss warning signs that an individual might be headed for a relapse.
- Describe the impact of the relapse process upon thinking and behavior.
- Describe the escalation of the phases of relapse, and explain how higher processes build upon the previous.

Introduction

As this is a text on the treatment of addiction, it is important that everyone be aware of a common pattern that many addicts experience. The purpose of this portion of the text is to assist the therapist in identifying indicators of regression so that the client will be able to address them and begin to move forward again. Additionally, armed with knowledge of the relapse process, the recovering individual may be able to thwart their own relapse.

Terence Gorski

The majority of those who work in the field of addiction recovery are familiar with the work of Terence Gorski. He is best known for his work on **relapse prevention**, specifically a relapse prevention program called CENAPS. Gorski is the author of several books on substance and codependence and is a frequent lecturer, and his relapse prevention programs have been recognized by the **National Institute on Drug Abuse (NIDA)**. His work on identifying the relapse process came from over 20 years of clinical and research experience working with chronic alcoholics.

Some of Terence Gorski's most profound work is on the relapse process. This work first appeared in his popular and well-received book *Staying Sober* (Gorski & Miller, 1986). He continued refining this work and eventually identified 11 stages of relapse. The beginning stage is common, and everyone in recovery will enter this stage and possibly others. It is often said in 12-step meetings that "you are either moving away from a drink or a drug or toward one." Recovery has been compared to walking up a down escalator. There is no room for complacency. But at the same time, everyone may backslide at some point during the course of their recovery. It has even been said that relapse often starts before the consumption of a substance.

Phases of Relapse

The following are Gorski's 11 phases of relapse, briefly defined:

Phase 1—**Internal Change**
During this common phase, there are changes in thinking, feeling, and behaving. Those in early recovery may believe the recovery program isn't as significant as other aspects in life. The client may have mild mood swings. The client may have stopped doing the things that have been working for him in the past.

Phase 2—**Return of Denial**
In this phase, the client may have a dull feeling that something is wrong but can't identify it. Because the recovering person cannot find a cause, or because he or she feels this change is insignificant, he or she may deny anything is wrong.

Phase 3—**Avoidance and Defensiveness**
The individual in this phase avoids most of those close enough to him/her that can identify that he or she is regressing. The recovering person may use justifications such as, "They'll just tell me to make more meetings." When the client is confronted about noticed changes, she or he becomes defensive and may argue and defend the decisions and/or choices that she or he is making. The client stops listening, as she or he is busy defending. Some of the indicators Gorski identified include believing substances will never be used again (as a result of having "learned the lesson"), worrying about others and taking their inventory, being defensive and not discussing what is going on, **compulsivity** (acting compulsively, e.g., cleaning, talking incessantly about minor things,

working too much), and returning to **impulsive behaviors** (acting without much thought).

Phase 4—**Crisis Building**

During this phase, problems are multiplying, and it is difficult to recognize why. An unconscious process may be lending itself to the situation, resulting in poor decision-making and mistakes. This is also made possible through warning signs like **tunnel vision**, where perception is restricted and the cause and effect of a decision is unclear. This can result in minor depression. As problems are arising and one is becoming mildly depressed, they may lose the ability to plan constructively. Then plans begin to fail. This leads to the next stage.

Phase 5—**Immobilization**

Feeling trapped by circumstances that seem beyond one's control, one feels like nothing can be solved. Daydreaming and wishful thinking are commonplace, as the relapsing individual hopes for things to get better but believes himself or herself unable to enact change. An immature wish to be happy from some magical cure (finding the perfect mate, winning the lottery, obtaining an amazing new job) replaces realistic planning and work.

Phase 6—**Confusion and Overreaction**

This phase is identifiable by cognitive and emotional difficulties. These include difficulty thinking clearly, difficulty managing feelings and emotions, difficulties with memory, periods of confusion, and difficulty managing stress. This leads to becoming frustrated and easily angered. Then, relationships with those who can help continue to deteriorate. Irritation with friends, partners, sponsors, and other support people are common.

Phase 7—**Depression**

It seems the natural result of some of the difficulties noted above would be depression. The typical symptoms of depression are obvious: change in sleep patterns, sleeping too much or too little, irregular eating habits, a lack of motivation or state of lethargy, and difficulties in maintaining daily structure. This also results in periods of deep depression, which cannot be denied.

Phase 8—**Behavioral Loss of Control**

In this phase, the recovering person often behaves in a manner that others would identify as "out of control" but is still unwilling to admit there is a serious issue despite the evidence. According to Gorski, some common warning signs are irregular attendance at 12-step meetings and/or therapy, an "I don't care" attitude, open rejection of help, dissatisfaction with life, and feelings of powerlessness and helplessness.

Phase 9—Recognition of Loss of Control

Denial of all of the above breaks in this phase, and the individual recognizes his life is spiraling out of control. However, as a result of the above phases, he has often isolated himself from those who can and will help and may avoid admitting to others the severity of the issue as a result of pride and feelings of shame. This phase is marked by self-pity, an increase in physical accidents or clumsiness as a result of overwhelming thoughts and feelings, thoughts of social use to escape the problem temporarily, a return to conscious lying, and a vast decrease in self-confidence, resulting in the belief the individual cannot experience recovery.

Phase 10—Option Reduction

In this phase, hope is dwindling, and the individual begins to believe the only options are substance use, suicide, or going insane. Some common hallmarks of this phase are unreasonable resentment (resenting others because they are happy is an example), a discontinuation of any program (treatment or 12-step attendance), overwhelming feelings of loneliness, frustration, stress, and anger, and a continued decrease in the ability to control thoughts, feelings, and behavior.

Phase 11—Substance Use

The relapse is official. The individual uses substances, either in a planned binge or an attempt to use socially for release. Either way, the result is disappointment, guilt, shame, and remorse. This contributes to a further loss of control with the substances, and the addiction cycle of substance use returns. As a result, life and health problems return or are exacerbated.

Evan was a 24-year-old Italian American male. He was a member of a recovery group. Weeks after the lecture on these phases and warning signs was covered, Evan exhibited the beginning signs of relapse. Both the group members and the therapist challenged him, but their efforts were ineffective. It seemed as though Evan lacked awareness of his process and didn't quite grasp what was happening with him. The therapist reviewed a pamphlet written by Gorski with Evan for a few minutes following a group session. The therapist highlighted the warning signs he and the group members had witnessed and the reasons why they believed Evan was headed for a relapse. Evan was taken aback, became open to the suggestion he might be headed for a relapse, and committed to making changes to prevent it.

Summary

An understanding of Gorski's phases and warning signs of relapse can be of unmitigated assistance for both the client and the therapist in helping a client prevent a relapse. The phases and signs assist in identifying a client who is headed for relapse, and even alone they can be sufficient in motivating the client toward a different course of action. Gorski, in this vein, has identified typical and general patterns of thinking and behavior that an individual engages in prior to actually picking up a substance again. It is beneficial to both the therapist and the client to be aware of these warning signs, and it can help the client to be receptive to challenges when they fall into these phases.

Key Terms

Relapse prevention

National Institute on Drug Abuse (NIDA)

Internal Change

Return of Denial

Avoidance and Defensiveness

Compulsivity

Impulsive behaviors

Tunnel vision

Immobilization

Confusion and Overreaction

Depression

Behavioral Loss of Control

Recognition of Loss of Control

Option Reduction

Substance Use

CHAPTER NINE

Relapse Prevention

Learning Objectives

- Understand the basics of the relapse prevention process.
- Identify the three essentials of relapse prevention and recovery.
- Describe the two types of reservations in recovery.
- Understand how triggers impact the recovery process.
- Demonstrate how to create a relapse prevention plan.

Introduction

A proper relapse prevention plan is critical in the recovery process. Anticipating relapse does not suggest a prediction of failure; rather, it indicates a realistic understanding of addiction. Fundamentally, every relapse prevention plan must cover necessary basics: abstinence, 12-step meeting attendance, participation in therapy, avoiding triggers. Honesty, open-mindedness, and willingness are essential for the recovery process. Taking an approach of humility positions the individual to have a greater chance of success. Of course, the process is not without its expected roadblocks. Reservations are typically present in the addict, which can hinder his progress. Expecting to be fearful or concerned about success and failure should be folded into the process. As those fears surface, prepared actions to mitigate those fears will hasten the onset of relapse. Ultimately, developing a plan that describes the likelihood of triggers and what to do when they are encountered will position the individual to have a greater chance of long-term recovery.

The Basics

Relapse prevention and the recovery process are not mutually exclusive. Depending on the therapist's view on addiction treatment, recovery and relapse prevention are one and the same, while others may feel they are not. The authors intentionally describe these processes as separate since it speaks to differing psychological mindsets of the client, as well as differing stages in their cessation of substance use.

This discussion of relapse prevention makes two assumptions: first, the client's goals are based on an abstinence-only program, and second, the client is doing the basics of recovery. These basics include complete abstinence (no use of mood-altering chemicals); attending 12-step meetings as frequently as recommended for the client's length of sobriety; sharing in the meetings; working the steps; working with a sponsor, and if in formal treatment, a therapist; using sober support; and applying knowledge gained in treatment to recovery. Additionally, this discussion assumes that, as much as possible, the client will avoid people, places, and things that are associated with his or her addiction. This discussion also assumes that new people, places, interests, and hobbies have become a part of the individual's life.

The Three Essentials

Three additional essentials that aid in recovery and relapse prevention include honesty, open-mindedness, and willingness, as are often emphasized by 12-step programs.

Honesty

Honesty includes the ability to be truthful, not only with others, but also with oneself. It is also attaining the insight to recognize and challenge rationalizations, justifications, and other cognitive distortions. Another aspect of honesty is the ability to recognize and share emotions. Additionally, the ability to be open and forthcoming with others, especially those with whom one is close, is essential. It includes the ability to question oneself and especially one's motivations for actions in any given situation. Another aspect of honesty includes getting past images, facades, or self-projections, which are designed to control how others view us, and sharing one's true, natural, authentic self with another.

Open-Mindedness

Open-mindedness is essential in recovery and relapse prevention. It includes humility. **Humility** is the ability for the former substance user to truly accept that he may not know what is best for him at any given moment. It is the ability to truly accept feedback, to be fully aware that others' perceptions may be more accurate than self-perception. This is of utmost importance when considering the phases and warning signs of relapse. Further, it is necessary when submitting oneself to the requirements of relapse prevention: attending 12-step meetings, abstinence, and the most difficult of all, letting go of any person (friend or family member) who enabled or encouraged the substance use. This will be a challenge for most because much of what they will be doing is reconstructing their entire lives. Resistance occurs because clients feel they can handle themselves adequately without making these sacrifices. However, this is where the tenet of "letting go" surfaces. Hand in hand with open-mindedness is trust. Trust in the professionals who are guiding the addict and trust in self that the person can have the discipline and strength to follow through with what is instructed for recovery. Many ask during and at the conclusion of educational groups based on that chapter, "What do I do if I'm unaware that I am in a relapse phase?" The only answer to that question is that the client must become aware that she or he is in a relapse phase. How does one become aware? This question has two possible answers. The first was stated in the previous paragraphs and consists of applying information gained in therapy and educational groups, and applying it for honest self-evaluation. This alone is often not enough for even the most diligently self-evaluative person. That is where open-mindedness comes in; one needs to be humble and evaluate the feedback received from others without becoming defensive.

Willingness

The third foundation is **willingness**. An individual, being honest with self and others and open-minded to others' feedback, must be willing to make the necessary changes in thinking and behavior. This may seem simple, but to borrow a saying from AA, "This is a simple program, not an easy one." Addicts often want the way they feel to change, but when told what they need to do to facilitate the change, they find excuses or otherwise balk at the necessary action. Willingness is therefore essential to prevent a relapse. It is the therapist's job to assist the client in moving through the stages of change. To do so, they must help the client increase his willingness. This can be done through motivation, providing hope, and helping the client explore his obstacles. Father Joseph Martin (www.fathermartinsashley.org), a priest famous for his work in the field of addiction, once said, "It is true you can lead a horse to water but you can't make him drink. It is your job to make him thirsty."

Reservations

A consideration that is often heard as a precursor to relapse, but seldom discussed, is that of reservations. A reservation can be defined in two ways: The first is as an appointment to use (similar to a hotel reservation). In this case, a person might say something like, "If my mom dies, I will most certainly use drugs." The second definition is that of a misgiving (similar to an uncertainty). One might say, "I have some reservations regarding his testimony." In this case, it refers to the individual withholding a judgment or decision regarding something he wants to think about longer or with more deliberation. In relation to recovery from substance use, **reservations** suggest that the person wasn't completely committed to abstinence. He still had misgivings regarding what he would do for recovery or how much stress he could handle before using. It is perfectly normal for a recovering person to have some reservations about substance use in early recovery. Despite it being normal, it still demonstrates an area for growth and needs to be addressed.

There are two categories of reservations identified in addiction recovery.

Type 1—Future Success

The first and most pervasive reservation, **future success**, is the belief that at some point in the future, the substance user will be able to successfully use drugs. A variation of this is the belief that he or she may not use drugs successfully, but that he or she will successfully recover from addiction at a later date. This latter type of reservation is encountered most often when working with adolescents, although it is encountered with adults as well. Despite adolescents' awareness that their drug use was "out of control," many hold the belief that they could use until it becomes worse—often much worse—and then they would enter recovery. The pitfalls of this philosophy are that most active adult addicts believed they would recover later in life as well (and didn't) and that many young people die as a result of their drug use.

Type 2—Situational Reservation

The second type of reservation, **situational reservation**, is one in which the substance user believes that if any one of the particular situations arose, he or she would pick up drugs or alcohol.

Overwhelming Emotions

When an addict is faced with a situation that to him or her feels unbearable emotionally, he or she would most likely resort to drug or alcohol use to cope with the emotions. The most common emotional reservation is grief due to the loss of a close relationship or a relationship for which someone entered recovery. Common thoughts associated with this are "I can't go on" or "I see no sense in staying sober or clean without this person in my life."

Stipulation

Another reservation of this type is one in which a stipulation is the reason for being in recovery. A common example of this is a legal stipulation. If the addict believes she or he will use drugs or alcohol once probation or parole is over, she or he will have this type of reservation. Conversely, if the substance-dependent person holds the belief that he would use drugs and alcohol if he were found guilty of a crime and sentenced to jail, he is entertaining this type of reservation. This is true whether he believes this relapse would happen in jail or prior to surrendering to the authorities.

Of Little Consequence

A final type of this reservation is one in which the addict believes she or he will use drugs or alcohol when one's use can no longer reap severe consequences to her or his life. One example of this is if the substance-dependent person were to instantly become a multimillionaire. Bills would be paid, no struggle would be necessary to obtain daily consumption, and most problems could have money thrown at them. Of course, potential medical problems and overdose would remain an issue, but many who entertain this reservation minimize these possible consequences. Another example of this type of reservation is returning to drug or alcohol use once retired. The person may picture himself retired with any children grown, a guaranteed retirement income coming in to pay what's left of his bills, and little to do besides kick back on the porch, relax, and chill while smoking marijuana (or using other substances).

Considerations

It is important to consider any reservations the substance user might have when developing the relapse prevention plan. When considering reservations, several areas must be explored. How reality based (likely to happen) is the reservation? For example, the odds are pretty slim of becoming an instant multimillionaire or of being plucked out of one's routine and found guilty of a crime that one did not commit. Although reservations in early recovery are normal and expected, it still indicates a weak area in recovery. A second consideration is the time span for the reservation. How far in the future would the reservation take effect? For example, the reservation about retirement occurred when the person was around 23 years old. Since retirement was at least 40 years or so away, the reservation was not immediately threatening to his recovery. Still, it indicates a weakness in recovery. Weaknesses are quite normal with less than a couple of years of recovery. Often recovery strengthens, and even if the reservation event occurs, abstinence is maintained. Even though these reservations are normal and often are not immediately threatening to recovery, a therapist should explore them and their meaning with the recovering person. Finally, if the likelihood of the reservation event occurring is substantial (as in the loss of a loved one, the breakup of a relationship, the end of legal stipulation, or being incarcerated for charges pending), it should be included in the relapse prevention plan and discussed thoroughly in therapy.

Triggers

Feelings as Triggers

Another guideline is to focus on internal triggers. Feelings are as important a relapse trigger as any and are often a predominant factor in a relapse. For example, anger is an emotion that can lead to a relapse. Other feelings that can contribute to relapse are grief, rejection, hurt, boredom, being stressed or overwhelmed, grandiosity, and arrogance. Even feelings that are normally considered positive, such as joy, happiness, and camaraderie, can be relapse triggers. When listing triggers, it is essential to consider these internal states.

FIGURE 9.1. Triggers aren't just limited to people (old friends, acquaintances, etc.), places (bars, shooting galleries, etc.), and things (music, paraphernalia, etc.); they are also feelings, moods and characteristics.

Character Traits as Triggers

Another internal state to consider is the client's character traits and his or her associated feelings and behavior. Often, character traits lead to a relapse. For a perfectionist, failing to attain perfection can contribute to a relapse. This is also true of people pleasing, promiscuity, rebelliousness, and false pride, to name a few. Exploration of character traits as triggers can help identify whether a plan needs to be developed to cope with it appropriately while working to change it into a positive character trait.

Developing the Plan

This brings us to the main focus of this chapter, developing a relapse prevention plan. It is necessary in recovery to identify relapse triggers and to develop a detailed, reasonable, workable plan to address these triggers. As a rule, the triggers should be specific to the client. In other words, the client simply saying "people, places, and things"—although triggers—are not an effective example because they are too general. A better example would be "Joe Sixpack is a trigger because we had a lot of good times together using drugs, and I have always had a hard time saying no to him." This example identifies a specific trigger.

Maxine is a 27-year-old African American female. She is a recovering addict, four years sober. Maxine was addicted to cocaine. At this point, she is considered to be the "perfect" recoverer by her peers. She attends two support groups a week, NA and AA. She attends individual psychotherapy once every two weeks. She has a full-time job, and she runs as a hobby. However, what most people don't know about Maxine is that she is a perfectionist. She must always "be the best." Insight was achieved early on in therapy when she realized why she "loved coke." She shared that it made her get everything done, and she did it well. This brought upon an added layer of euphoria that she experienced outside of the drug. Maxine's daily struggle is to work on this perfectionistic tendency. When her peers call her "perfect," it triggers her to "not fail." Maxine's journey exemplifies the importance of character traits. She is aware of her tendencies and makes a daily effort to not give in.

The same specificity applies to making the relapse prevention plan for each trigger. For the client to say "I'll call my sponsor" in response to a trigger is a poor plan. Is it always possible that he will be able to stop everything and call his sponsor? Is it reasonable to believe that a sponsor will always be there to take the call? What if the sponsor is unavailable or isn't able to provide the best answer to that particular situation? These questions typify why it is vital to make a reasonable, workable, detailed plan of action as a response to encountering a relapse trigger. Although one action step may be phoning a sponsor, alone it is insufficient.

Before moving to an example of a relapse prevention plan, we want to add that it has been our experience that when a relapse occurs, it can be attributed to one of two major reasons:

A rationalization or a series of rationalizations, which lead the addict to believe that drug or alcohol use is the most viable option. Examples in this category include people pleasing, feelings of grief or boredom, and **terminal uniqueness** (the belief that what has worked for others in recovery is not necessary for the addict because she or he is different).

Apathy toward the consequences of a relapse, which leads to an "I-don't-care-what-happens-to-me" attitude (often called "the fuck-its"). Examples in this category include anger and rage, depression, and hopelessness.

It is critical to understand that either of these types of relapses can be avoided by identifying the personal triggers (as well as warning signs) that lead to a relapse and by developing an appropriate, well-thought-out plan.

The following is an example of a relapse prevention plan for one particular relapse trigger. Please pay attention to the detail of the plan and how it addresses possible stumbling blocks to the second action step of the plan. When making a plan, it is helpful to include utilization of sober support, distraction, avoidance, and other therapeutic techniques you may have learned and practiced, such as cognitive challenges, relaxation, guided imagery meditation, or desensitization. There are examples of both cognitive challenges and systematic desensitization in the following example of a relapse prevention plan. Finally, use your imagination; be creative in making your plan.

Example:

Trigger	* Music by the Grateful Dead
Why	* Their music glorifies drug use
	* Memories of good times I had getting high to their music or at their concerts
Plan	* Do not listen to my Grateful Dead CDs (maybe even get rid of them).
	* Avoid stations that play this music.
	* When memories arise, remember bad times (bad trips, getting ill, not remembering the concert, getting arrested) that also happened.
	* If unable to avoid their music, begin listening to it in moderation when in a social setting not involving drugs or alcohol.

> * If I hear it and memories cause craving, I will call my sponsor and go through my list of other sober support people.
>
> * If unable to utilize sober support, play music with no associations or otherwise distract myself until I can share with someone.

Summary

The relapse prevention plan is a significant yet often neglected aspect of addiction recovery. In developing an effective relapse prevention plan, there are many aspects that must be considered. The individual should be aware of the basics of recovery (12-step meeting attendance, participation in therapy, avoiding people one used with). Honesty, open-mindedness, and willingness are considered by many to be essential to addiction recovery. In addition to these aspects, reservations regarding substance use are important to explore. We have identified the different types of reservations in this chapter to help spur this discussion. Finally, it is of utmost importance that the plan be detailed, reasonable, and workable for the person in addiction recovery. Individualized and specific plans are crucial to increasing the chances of success.

Key Terms

Honesty	Willingness	Situational reservation
Open-mindedness	Reservations	Terminal uniqueness
Humility	Future success	

CHAPTER TEN

Romantic Relationships in Early Recovery

Learning Objectives

- Discuss the different types of love identified by Robert Sternberg's model.
- Explain why falling in love and entering new romantic relationships can be detrimental to early recovery.
- Describe how casual, noncommitted sex may negatively impact recovery efforts.
- Identify unconscious aspects that go into attraction and partnering.
- Explain how attraction and partnering might be detrimental to early recovery efforts and to lasting relations.
- Discuss the impact and dynamics of self-esteem that affect attraction and partnering.
- Discuss how family dynamics in an alcoholic/addicted home relate to attraction and partnering.

Introduction

As many addiction therapists have heard, (and probably said), it is detrimental in early recovery for the person to become involved in romantic relationships. Perhaps it is first necessary to define *romantic relationships*. **Romantic** refers to experiencing feelings of attraction, infatuation, or what the individual considers love. **Relationship** refers to ongoing or regular contact between an individual or individuals who are experiencing these romantic feelings. This chapter will describe some of the reasons why romantic relationships are detrimental to early recovery and some of the pitfalls that await those who attempt them.

It is important to share a few words about the expectations of this chapter. First, this chapter discusses attraction and romantic feelings, and attempts to bring logic to what many consider a magical experience. Your authors, however, attempt to elaborate on what Carl G. Jung stated: "Until you make the unconscious conscious, it will direct your life and you will call it fate." Despite whatever logic one might possess, humans are emotionally driven people, and all of the logic in the world often has no effect on one's decisions when experiencing a strong emotion like love (or infatuation).

Love

Love is a difficult concept to define. It is usually referred to as an emotion and has also been described as a behavior. Both are accurate and are not mutually exclusive. If you experience the emotion of love, it stands to reason that you would behave accordingly. Nearly everyone agrees that there are different types of love as expressed to different people. There is love for a child, parent, sibling, friend, and lover. For the purpose of this section, we will concern ourselves only with love between partners. According to social psychologist Robert Sternberg (1988), there are four types of love in relation to partners. The diagram below describes them and their three components.

Carolina is a 19-year-old Colombian female who moved to Florida at the age of four. Steven is a 22-year-old Caucasian male who was born and raised in New Jersey. Carolina and Steven met in NA. Carolina is three months sober from prescription drugs, and Steven is two weeks sober from marijuana. Carolina and Steven were drawn to each other immediately at the meetings. They were close in age and both were isolated (by their own doing) from the rest of the support group, despite many attempts from other members to draw them in. Carolina and Steven began meeting up for coffee before meetings and eventually after meetings. This continued for a few weeks until their first kiss. Riddled with guilt, but lifted with excitement, they spent many hours talking about the pros and cons of being in a relationship. Steven was able to recognize that Carolina might be just a "crutch" for him to get over using drugs. However, Carolina felt as though she was falling in love. After two months of dating, Carolina moved in with Steven. They kept their relationship a secret from the group members, as well as family members because of the known discouragement of relationships in early recovery. Despite it all, they forged ahead in their relationship. After three months of living together (a total of five months in the relationship), Steven began to distance himself from Carolina. He put a lot of effort into work and school and realized that he was not ready to be in a long-term, committed relationship. Carolina, on the other hand, was hoping for a marriage proposal within the year. After Steven expressed his feelings to Carolina, she grudgingly moved out. Steven felt guilty and increased his time in support groups and with his friends to help cope with the emotions. Carolina, after weeks of crying with no relief, began using prescription drugs to cope with the pain of the breakup.

As can be seen in the diagram, the three components of love are **intimacy,** which can be described as getting to know the person and liking what you know; **passion,** which is infatuation; and **commitment,** which is self-explanatory.

Intimacy combined with passion results in **romantic love.** This is what most partners experience in the beginning of a relationship, and it is usually energizing and exciting.

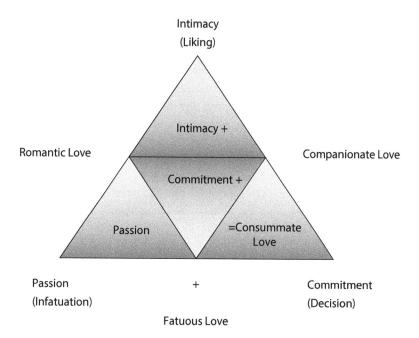

FIGURE 10.1. Sternberg's theory of love is often referred to as the triangle theory of love, as there are three components that combine for different types of love.

FIGURE 10.2. Romantic relationships can be a source of both support and stress. This is one reason getting into a romantic relationship in early recovery is ill-advised.

Intimacy combined with commitment results in **companionate love**. This is what many relationships become after time. The partners are comfortable with one another, know each other well, and are committed to the relationship.

Passion or infatuation combined with commitment results in **fatuous love**. This is the result of getting swept up in passion and making a long-term commitment without really knowing the person.

Consummate love is when all three components—intimacy, passion, and commitment—are combined together. Of course, it is unrealistic to expect that the overwhelming passion present at the beginning of many relationships will continue forever. This type of passion varies in length, depending on the individuals. Most consummate relationships have passion that comes and goes and varies in intensity.

Many people confuse infatuation or passion with love. After a period of time together, and as the passion naturally cools, they find themselves falling out of love. This is where the saying "I love you, but I'm not in love with you any more" comes from. Many people then end up going from one romantic love relationship to another, wondering why they cannot find a "true love."

Given that the experience of love draws upon significant emotional resources, people in recovery are encouraged to keep a safe distance from the potential development of love. As unpredictable as life, love can easily spring itself upon a person. Once it has happened, how is someone in recovery supposed to say no? It is the experience of addiction counselors that once a person reveals that he is in love, it is almost impossible to extinguish the emotion. This explains why counselors are charged with identifying signs and situations that can lead a person to fall in love (those reasons are beyond the scope of this text).

Sex

When told it is ill advised to enter into a relationship, a great deal of addicts in early recovery ask the question, "Well, what about sex?" Usually, this refers to what is commonly called **friends with benefits** or **sport sex**: the act of sex for nothing more than the enjoyment of the act (no emotional involvement, no commitment, no strings). Although this seems cut and dried and mostly harmless if two consenting adults are involved, there are a few complications that at least should be considered. The first is that many people, let alone addicts in early recovery, have difficulty separating sex and intimacy. Often, feelings develop despite the belief that they never would.

Along these lines is the tendency of those who have been sexually abused to **sexualize intimacy**. This occurs when a friendship develops, secrets are shared, and a sexual attraction becomes apparent, even though none had existed prior to the friendship getting closer. Because of the high prevalence of sexual abuse among addicts and the nature of sharing on a personal level in the 12-step programs and groups, this is a very real and serious risk. To begin buddy sex may just be a symptom of diseased thinking and could prove very detrimental.

Another consideration is the effect of casual sex on self-esteem. Although some believe it is possible to have casual sex with no guilt or remorse, this is often not the case. Casual sex often goes against the morals and values that one was taught. Any time that we behave in a manner that goes against our morals, we experience guilt. Guilt can have a detrimental effect on self-esteem.

Even if it does not go against any morals or values that one possesses, it may likely be a behavior that was engaged in during active addiction. Since addiction and promiscuity often go hand in hand, having casual sex would tap into this addictive behavior. And even if an individual was not promiscuous during his addiction, behaving with an "I-want-what-I-want-when-I-want-it" attitude promotes addictive behavior.

Sylvia, a 29-year-old Mexican American female, has been in recovery for methamphetamine addiction. She struggled throughout her life with engaging in high-risk patterns of behavior (e.g., sky diving, swimming with sharks, motocross racing). When she was 26, she began a relationship with Marcel, who introduced her to meth. She was thrilled with the euphoric and erotic experiences. After reaching her bottom at age 28, she began multiple treatment modalities to help recover. Sylvia today realizes something she hadn't for the past year. She has increasingly engaged in "buddy sex" over the past year. She admits that she has had over 30 partners in the past seven months. Sylvia recognizes, only because of the number of partners, that this is excessive. However, she denies that it's a "problem." She shared that she loves the "thrill" and the "rush" of seducing an almost stranger. Has Sylvia moved from one addiction to another?

One way that self-esteem can be raised is by developing delayed gratification and making decisions that will make the person feel better in the long run. Not engaging in sport or buddy sex is an example of this.

Relationships

Most people believe in a spiritual or magical element that causes them to fall in love and enter into a relationship. Many believe there is a "soul mate" waiting for them and that fate can step in at any moment anywhere and deliver their soul mate to them. The words that follow are not attempts to demystify love and relationships but are simply meant to keep individuals from falling victim to other aspects that can appear to be mystifying.

Many people confuse projections of their ideal mate onto the person that they desire with having found their soul mate. A **projection** is an internal ideal, a thought process, or a state that is attributed to another person. In other words, the person knows what he wants and needs his ideal mate to be, and he places these attributes and qualities onto another individual. He then observes this other person's behavior and relates it to his ideal. If he does not recognize the projection, he may believe he has found his soul mate. Later, when he knows the person better, the other person begins to fall short of expectations. When the person falls short of expectations, often the search for a "real" soul mate begins again. This pattern of disappointment will continue until an individual realizes the reality of projection and does not give in to the fantasy that anyone can identify his or her soul mate early in a relationship.

Another aspect of relationships is the **bargaining process**. This is not an external event, but an internal one. Each person entering a relationship is aware of the attributes that he or she brings to the table. These can include attractiveness, financial security, a quality of sweetness, intelligence, being a giving person, being attentive, considerate, good in bed, and so forth. Knowing what attributes one brings to the table, the individual wants a comparable partner. This does not mean that we necessarily want someone exactly as attractive, nice, financially secure, for example, as we are. But it means that we want an equal or better bargain in line with what we value. For example, how many very attractive women have you seen with men who are financially secure? The man knows he brings financial well-being and security, and values an attractive trophy for a partner. The woman in this example knows she is very attractive and values financial security. This example is crude, but this does exist. The actual bargaining process is more complicated due to the many aspects to consider. So, if one accepts this bargaining component of relationships as true, one may wonder why it is a problem. After all, it exists whether in early recovery or not. The problem arises not due to the bargaining aspect alone. It arises because the bargaining aspect occurs while in early recovery.

Addicts do not enter recovery with healthy self-esteem. This affects their perception of what attributes they are bringing to the relationship bargaining table. This presents several problems. The first is that they are not look-

FIGURE 10.3. Because addicts often enter treatment with low self-esteem, they don't see themselves or their potential accurately, and this affects their potential relationships.

ing for or getting much in the bargain for a partner. If they do not feel very good about themselves, or if their belief that they feel good about themselves is instead a defense mechanism, they will not expect much in return for what they bring.

Another problem that is in line with this is that during the first year of recovery, a great deal of growth should occur. This growth raises self-esteem, and if one entered a relationship early in recovery, they would now realize that they can do better. Additionally, even if both grow and both of the partners' self-esteem rises, it is likely they will grow apart.

Family dynamics in early childhood also affect what we look for or are attracted to in a mate. One example of this is evident in the dynamics of the alcoholic home. As we will cover in the chapter on addiction as a family disease, the Family Hero role is usually attracted to a dependent personality, such as a Lost Child or Mascot role. This also occurs in homes where there has been abuse. Often, the daughter of a father who was abusive to the mother will end up in a relationship with a man who is abusive, even if there was no indication of him being abusive. Similarly, the daughter of an alcoholic often ends up married to an alcoholic. These examples illustrate the power of unconscious attraction. Until these issues or complexes are sufficiently resolved, individuals run the risk of falling victim to them and ending up in bad relationships.

Another consideration regarding relationships is the impact of socialization on what we find attractive. Statistically, most people marry within their own race, religion, socioeconomic status, and culture. We tend to form close bonds with those in close proximity to us regularly. Generally, those who are like us, culturally surround us. We meet people at school or college, at jobs, at events we enjoy, at places in our neighborhoods. As such, we stay predominantly within our culture. Where we meet people is also where we find potential partners. This demonstrates not only the power of proximity in attraction, but also supports the idea we are attracted to those most like us in important ways.

For those entering addiction recovery, this can be quite an obstacle. Meeting someone new is exciting, and it is comforting to find someone who seems to understand you. But for the person in recovery, this often equates to someone with either substance issues or codependency issues. It is easy to see how this can confound one's own recovery efforts.

A final consideration in regard to relationships in early recovery is that those in this stage of recovery rarely know who they really are and often battle with this concept. If they are unsure of who they are, how can they know what they will want in a relationship? If they do not know who they are, they cannot truly love themselves. If they do not love themselves, how can they love a partner?

In light of these considerations on the topic of early recovery and relationships, everyone considering entering a relationship has reason for concern. The question "Is it possible this attraction is due to unconscious complexes or addictive behavior?" must be asked and strongly considered.

With all this said, those with a psychodynamic background believe that the solution to unhealthy attraction is not simply overcoming it cognitively but forming ever-healthier relationships, including one with a therapist. As Thomas Lewis and Fari Amini and Richard Lannon proclaim in their book, *A General Theory of Love*, "A person cannot choose to desire a certain kind of relationship, any more than he can will himself to ride a unicycle" (2000, p. 175). Instead, it is suggested that the therapeutic relationship begins to bring about small changes that accumulate and bring the individual closer to healthy relations.

Summary

There are several old sayings in addiction recovery about relationships, and they are derogatory: "Two sickies don't make a wellie," "Two dead batteries won't start a car," and, the point of this chapter, "Don't get in a relationship for the first year of recovery." In truth, few follow this maxim. Not getting into a relationship is easier said than done.

There are many good reasons for the newly recovering individual to avoid getting into a new relationship in early recovery. Love is difficult to define, can be unpredictable, and has many factors which contribute to it. Love draws on a great deal of emotional energy. Love can skew an individual's perception of reality, making it rose colored. Who needs to work in therapy when life is so good due to newfound love? Attraction, a cornerstone of romantic love, is one of the confounding factors of love. People rarely question where love and attraction come from. Hopefully, with the use of this chapter and some self-exploration, the counselor and the recovering individual can explore the process and pitfalls before they put the recovering individual at risk.

Key Terms

Romantic	Commitment	Friends with benefits
Relationship	Romantic love	Sport sex
Love	Companionate love	Sexualize intimacy
Intimacy	Fatuous love	Projection
Passion	Consummate love	Bargaining process

CHAPTER ELEVEN

Addiction as a Family Disease

Learning Objectives

- Understand the relationship between family behaviors and addiction.
- Define the different behaviors that can develop in a family affected by addiction.
- Describe the relationship between family roles and addiction.
- Define the different types of roles in the family of the addicted.
- Understand the impact family therapy can have on addiction.

Introduction

Your authors maintain that addiction is a family disease. This suggests two things: addiction has a tremendous impact on the family of the addict, and family dynamics play a major role in the development and perpetuation of an addiction.

Addiction is a situation that affects the whole family unit; whether the addict is the parent, partner, or child, the addiction has its effect. Yet it is not uncommon to place sole responsibility for change on the addicted individual. The addicted individual becomes the "identified patient," the one who needs the help and who needs to change. In actuality, it is beneficial for anyone involved with the addict to change their behavior. These changes benefit both the person and the addict.

First, it is essential to explain how addiction affects the family unit. The most obvious ways that the addiction affects the family is in negative feelings that arise. Often, these feelings are the result of unmet expectations. No matter what role the addict plays in the family—father, mother, caregiver, son, daughter,

FIGURE 11.1. Addiction negatively affects members of the family, and the health of family members may suffer.

sibling, or grandparent—there are expectations of that role. These expectations are seldom met by the addict. These unmet expectations, whether placed on the addict directly by the family or assumed because of societal norms, lead to feelings of hurt and anger in the nonaddicted family members.

A way in which the family's feelings can be affected by the addict is due to the shame and guilt of parents thinking they did something wrong in raising their child. This shame or guilt can result in projected anger toward the addict or overprotection of other children.

Siblings can also experience jealousy when parents treat the addicted sibling differently. This can result in additional responsibilities and/or stricter rules to be followed.

If a parent is the addicted family member, the resulting feeling in the child or children may be shame. This is usually due to the unpredictable or irrational behavior of the parent. Children of addicts can experience embarrassment at their parent's public behavior as well.

Another way that feelings in the family are affected is due to a battle for control. Nonaddicted family members often erroneously believe that they can somehow help the addict by controlling them. There are several ways that this is demonstrated, and all can also be considered enabling behaviors.

Family Behaviors

Enabling—Any behavior which softens the consequences of an addict's behavior.

Enabling can take several different forms. The first resembles becoming a savior. This type believes they can help if they just find the right formula for the addict. Essentially, the savior feels that he can rescue the addict from his problems. Another type of enabler is the one who believes he cannot leave or abandon the addict in his or her time of need. He believes the addict would become worse if he were to withdraw support, be it emotional or financial.

Another effect that addiction has on a family is through codependency. Although many of the above-stated enabling behaviors could constitute a codependent relationship, it is important to define it here.

Codependency—When a person relies on an (addicted) individual for emotional and psychological well-being. When an individual's self worth is determined by his relationship with another.

FIGURE 11.2. Enabling is described as an act that softens the consequences of an addict's behavior. Additionally, some view it as fostering the addiction in some way.

Codependency can occur in any relationship between an addict and another individual. It is most common, however, in romantic relationships. It is also a difficult dependency to break. Frequently, so much self-worth is invested in protecting, supporting, being martyred by, and taking responsibility for the addict that there is an unconscious drive to keep the status quo. Further, there is gratification occurring for the partner—usually emotional—that perpetuates the behavior; thus, "co"dependency. This unconscious drive can continue to occur into the addict's recovery from chemical dependency. It can become visible through what can be described as sabotaging behaviors toward the addict by some or all of their family members. Examples of this would be drinking in front of the addict or alcoholic, encouraging the addict to accompany a family member to a bar, or statements like "I liked you better when you were using."

These sabotaging behaviors often occur because the addiction and eventual recovery (if it occurs) have altered the homeostasis, or balance, of the family. As an addict fails to fill the family role and its subsequent responsibilities, other family members adjust to fulfil those responsibilities. For example, if the father is the addict, the mother may leave the home to work and may become the financial support for the family. She may become responsible for writing checks to pay the bills. The eldest child may take on child-rearing responsibilities and other household duties, such as cooking and laundry. They may also handle the disciplining of the other children. In this example, the balance of the family responsibilities has changed to compensate for an absent member (the addict).

As a result of this shift in balance, family members become identified with their new and additional roles, and it is likely their self-worth grows. If the addict enters recovery, there often is a resistance to relinquish new roles and their rewards (martyrdom, self-worth, responsibilities, freedoms).

Family Roles

Parentification

A potential and common result of the shift in homeostasis that occurs in addicted families is parentification of children. **Parentification** occurs when a child takes on adult-like roles in the family. Again, this can occur without there being addiction in the family. Another common time this occurs is during a divorce. Often, the newly single parents will rely more heavily on an older child to help with the other children in the family or with chores around the home.

In a family where a parent is addicted, this still occurs as the adult abandons his or her responsibilities. Someone must fill the parental role, and this is often one of the oldest children, especially a female child. In most writings on the effects of substance use on a family, credit is given to Sharon Wegscheider-Cruse in her work on "family survival roles." In her book *The Family Trap: No One Escapes From a Chemically Dependent Family*, Wegscheider-Cruse identifies the family system concepts in addiction and explores the roles in the family that develop as a result. However, as Peter L. Meyers points out in his review of *Chemical Dependency: A Family Affair*, an excellent text by Olivia Curtis (1999) on how addiction affects the family, these roles have been discussed well before Wegscheider-Cruse by family psychology masters like Adler and Minuchin. Regardless, these roles are simplified and generalized here.

Family Hero

The addiction of a parent often results in common roles in an addicted family. The parentified child often takes on the role of the **Family Hero**. The outward behavior of the Family Hero is typically that of a perfectionist: he is parentified, a people pleaser, overly responsible, and works at being good enough. Working at being good enough is a result of some of the inward feelings, which include hurt feelings, feeling inadequate, feeling guilt, fear, and confusion, and low self-esteem. No matter what the Family Hero's accomplishments, he never feels good enough.

The family unit gains from each of the roles that will be discussed. In the case of the Family Hero, the family is provided someone to be proud of, a member who gives the family self-worth and a sense of normality.

Scapegoat

Another role common to the addicted family is that of the **Scapegoat.** Contrary to popular vernacular, the Scapegoat is not simply someone to blame.

Instead, the Scapegoat relieves the tension in a dysfunctional family by attracting the negative attention to themselves. Sometimes the Scapegoat has tried the role of Family Hero, but eventually rebelled against it when continued feelings of inadequacy prevailed. Sometimes the role of Family Hero was already taken, and the Scapegoat, seeking equal attention, settled for negative attention. Regardless of the motivation, the Scapegoat draws the negative energy of the family to himself or herself. Often, the Scapegoat child in the family develops an addiction as well.

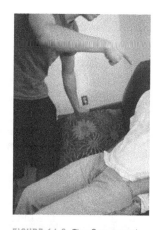

FIGURE 11.3. The Scapegoat role has been found to have a negative correlation with measures of family satisfaction, family strength and parent-adolescent communication.

Scapegoats are often perceived as hostile, defiant, withdrawn, and sullen. Often, they won't compete and instead settle into the role of troublemaker. This outward expression is often a result of the internal feelings of hurt and abandonment, as well as anger and rejection. The Scapegoat frequently feels totally inadequate and has no or very low self-worth.

Clown or Mascot

A third common role in the addicted family is that of the **Clown** or **Mascot**. The Clown or Mascot provides comic relief to the family and thereby reduces the tension. They often feel compelled to be cute and funny. They are often also perceived as immature, fragile, and needing protection. Sometimes they are hyperactive, anxious, and possibly even have a learning disability. Often, their internal feelings are that of fear and loneliness, inadequacy, the belief they are unimportant. Like other children in the addicted family, they suffer from low self-esteem. Usually, the Clown or Mascot surrounds himself with superficial friends, but this does not quell his loneliness.

Lost Child

The final child role in the addicted family is the **Lost Child**. The Lost Child is perceived as blending into the background. I can often identify a Lost Child in my group (in group therapy, members often resort to roles they held in their family of origin) by having difficulty remembering if that member was present that day or not. They are quiet, blend into the background, often lack emotion, and are perceived as quiet and shy. One problem that seems to be correlated is a tendency to overeat. The Lost Child provides a reward to the family by being one less child to worry about by providing no additional stress or worries.

Whenever a therapist discusses these roles with clients, he should ask if a person could have switched roles. This is an excellent question, and switching roles is more common than once thought. Many children will try to be the hero of the family but find the reward too little to maintain the role. Other times the role is already taken, and despite doing well, they do not excel as much as the other child. Unable to be the hero, many children resort to the role of scapegoat, which is also a powerful role in the family. Still other times, the oldest child, feeling outshined by a younger sibling, turns to another role.

Throughout our experience treating addiction, we have often found it very difficult to get the family into treatment. When families do attend, it is often simply to see what the addict is doing, find out how the recovering addict is progressing, and to see if they are being blamed! Although they certainly believe they want the addict to stop using, they do not want to take responsibility for their role in the family member's addiction.

Family therapy is about seeing the system (the family system as the patient), not just the person addicted. Systems theory holds that the addiction did not develop in a vacuum; everyone played a part, and continues to do so, in perpetuating the addiction. The answer is not to simply address the addict but to rectify faulty communication and interaction patterns and roles that perpetuate the substance problem.

We have always found family therapy beneficial in many respects. Even if faulty behavioral patterns aren't rectified, education can be garnered and some insight might be gained. Additionally, there is always the possibility that the family will engage in therapy and emerge healthier.

Family Therapy

Family therapy has much to offer in addiction treatment. There are several ways family therapy can be utilized for the treatment of addiction.

In family therapy, the family is the patient. The addicted family member is demonstrating the symptomatology, but it is a family system problem. Using traditional family therapy, the therapist would view the addiction as a symptom of a family problem, with everyone in the family system contributing to it. The addicted individual is no more the problem than anyone else.

Anthony is a Puerto Rican male who was approaching his 21st birthday. He participated in group therapy. In group therapy, he shared with the group that he was going to smoke marijuana and drink to celebrate his birthday. Anthony didn't feel that this was much of a slip because he had kicked opiates. As his treatment drew to a close, he continued to drink and use cannabis regularly. During group process, he had made a comment to the group that he doesn't feel substance use twice a week constitutes a loss of control. The group had a reaction to this but recognized that Anthony had made progress by refraining from opiate use.

As the end of treatment approached, his commitment to only using twice a week was in place. However, when Anthony attended what turned out to be his last group, he reported using four times that previous week. He shared that his excessive substance use was okay because his father told him three or four times a week was acceptable. His father was like a friend to Anthony, and the mother was more like a parent to both. Additionally, Anthony made it clear before sharing what his father said that he did not want the mother to know this information, including that the father and son had used marijuana together recently. What is unfolding is a triangulation against the mother, as well as how the family unit is working to keep the individual sick. This is an excellent example of how the family system is the problem, not just the individual.

Although the family system theory offers excellent insights into the treatment of addiction, the system view need not be held vehemently when treating addiction. As discussed earlier in this book, addiction has many different contributing factors. Often, we find more than one contributor to be at play in the clients presenting for treatment. As such, we do completely give ourselves to the theory that it is singularly a family system issue. This is not to minimize the possible effect of the family system on addiction. As discussed in the previous chapter, often everyone in the family can play a role and can benefit from family therapy.

One excellent way family therapy can be utilized is as an adjunct to primary treatment for the addicted individual. While the person suffering with addiction is attending inpatient or outpatient therapy, the family can attend at least a few sessions as part of the treatment milieu. In these family sessions, family members can be educated about addiction and enabling, as well as their role in perpetuating the addiction.

It is key that the family of someone suffering with addiction be involved in treatment. One must be cognizant of the fact that often in addiction treatment, the individual suffering with addiction is advised to cut ties with those who have contributed to the addiction. Addicts are also advised to put themselves first and not to allow others to distract them from their purpose of maintaining abstinence. This will frequently impact the family negatively, which has felt the addict had been selfish while using. To the family, the newly recovering individual may be continuing his or her addictive behavior. This is where education about what to expect from someone new in recovery can be helpful. Continuing family therapy could facilitate the ability to address these types of issues.

Unfortunately, what often happens in addiction treatment is that the family identifies the person with the addiction as the only person with an issue and sees no need to engage in treatment. Sometimes this is a result of anger at the addict and not wanting some bleeding-heart therapist to take his side. At times it is out of fear of being blamed for the addiction. Sometimes, the family has its own guilt about behavior or contributing factors and does not want to be reminded of it. Other times, family members have been blamed so many times by the addicted individual that they don't want to hear any more. And on other occasions they are so disillusioned by previous attempts—and failures—at recovery that they don't want to get involved again. Regardless of the reasons (and there are many), the family does not want to engage in therapy. It can always be beneficial, however, to get the family involved.

There are benefits beyond the gaining of insight into the addiction and recovery process. Besides understanding how the family adjusts and reacts in an attempt to end or sometimes foster an addiction, another benefit of family therapy is support for the family. The family is able to receive support and gain understanding that what they are experiencing is normal.

Sometimes the person in addiction treatment does not want the family involved because he wants the option to fall back on old behaviors without catching slack from the family. He may also not want to let the family notice any indications of his relapse, as he knows it will negatively impact their lives. Many active addicts believe they will be able to right the ship quickly enough and want to be able to do so without the family knowing they slipped. Unfortunately, this often is not the case, and the active addict is unable to get back on track on his own. Addiction is a disease that affects thinking, and the thoughts discussed above are evidence of this. Again, this is another way the family can benefit from family therapy.

When confronted with someone in their family developing an addiction, one of the biggest difficulties for family members is the issue of control. This is especially true when the addicted family member is the child, and the parents struggle between what is enabling, what is controlling, and what the best balance is.

It is clearly difficult to decide what to do as a parent in these circumstances. Often, there is no clear-cut, correct answer. However, one of the most significant things to do in these cases is to set appropriate limitations and then stick to them.

Another way in which a family dynamic can be displayed is in relationships. Addicts have a way of bringing out the "parent" in their partner. What often occurs is the partner begins to take on the role of a parent and the addict that of the "bad" child. The circumstances mirror those of a parent with an addicted child; limits are set, broken, consequences often aren't followed through, and the cycle of lines being drawn and crossed continues.

> The J. family has an intact marriage and three grown children, two male and one female. The youngest two are fraternal twins, and the addicted individual is the female twin. She is in her early twenties and still lives at home, as do all of these adult children. She is addicted to marijuana and entered treatment as the result of an arrest. She has maintained abstinence from marijuana but has admitted to drinking excessively. As she appears to be trying to establish her own identity and also appears to be the current scapegoat in the family, she and her parents have engaged in family therapy.
>
> Her parents are very loving and supportive parents. Their love and support for their daughter are evident in the sessions, as well as their frustration with poor decisions she has made. The parents attempt to prevent her from further poor decision-making by not allowing her to engage in certain activities, such as celebrating her birthday in a hotel room with her friends. This restriction, naturally, caused the daughter to be very upset. Nonetheless, the parents feel they must be firm because in the past she has proven to have poor judgment (e.g., drinking while driving). The parents did compromise and allowed her to spend the night at a friend's house with a family they know well enough. The daughter appreciated their willingness to allow her to be on her own, but also realized she couldn't break "the rules" because she was in another family's home. Within a very short period of time, she was able to prove herself trustworthy to her parents.

It seems addicts learn early that the horrible things possible from addiction don't happen. They use a substance and find it wasn't as bad as the news, Drug Abuse Resistance Education (DARE), or parents and teachers had said. As the drug (or alcohol) takes a slow grip on their lives, many threats never materialize. Parents or partners threaten to throw them out or leave, but do not. Or they do, but it is temporary, and the addict—through promises, charm, manipulation, or genuine remorse—makes promises they won't keep but which get them back in the house. Although it can be a slow process and although there are exceptions to the rule, the addict learns many threats can be circumvented. This is part of the reason limitation and consequences must be followed through.

We have worked with families that try everything in order to get their loved one to stop using. Sometimes they tighten the reins, trying to reel in the addict. The addict frequently rebels further and sinks deeper into addiction. Sometimes they try providing more freedom. Many addicts will use the freedom to use substances even more and again sink further into addiction. Parents often try giving more responsibility so the addict will "grow up." The addict may use because he feels overwhelmed. Parents may relieve the responsibility, helping to manage money and helping financially. The addict may then use more regardless of this help as well. If this all sounds hopeless, you are hearing it correctly. The family has no control over the addict's behavior. All they have is some influence, and this needs to be consistent. It is best served with care and compassion, but not a bleeding heart. If this sounds confusing, again, it is. The balance is difficult, and often family therapy can be of assistance.

It is essential to understand that there is no clear-cut answer, no cookie-cutter treatment for the family battling addiction. Each is an individual case, just like every addict is an individual and deserves individualized treatment. The counselor's approach must start with knowledge and a theory and move toward what will work for the particular family in front of her or him. Although this can be unnerving, it is the best approach.

Summary

Many in the field of addiction treatment view addiction as a family problem. Terms such as *enabling* and *codependency* describe behaviors that are common in families with someone addicted to substances. When the parent is addicted, children often take on specific roles that persevere throughout their lifespan. These roles affect the way in which they interact with others, whom they are attracted to romantically, and how they function. Although family members can take on more than one role or can switch roles during the course of a lifetime, the addict in the family impacts their personalities. Whenever feasible, in addiction treatment, family therapy can be of vital assistance in the effort to beat addiction. At times, there is tremendous resistance by the family to engage in therapy. At times, the family may work against the recovering individual's efforts. Whatever the recovering individual's situation, it is beneficial to look at addiction as a systems issue and to address the system when able.

Key Terms

Enabling	Scapegoat	Clown or Mascot
Codependency		Lost child
Parentification		
Family hero		

CHAPTER TWELVE

Co-Occurring Disorders

Learning Objectives

- Understand the nature of schizophrenia and dual diagnosis.
- Explain the interplay between personality disorders and substance use.
- Identify the co-occurring nature of depression and substance use.
- Explain the relationship between anxiety disorders and substance use.

Introduction

When a person suffers from two diseases at the same time (typically a substance use disorder and mental health disorder), he is considered to have a **dual diagnosis**. Therapists frequently experience diagnostic difficulty when a person presents with a multitude of symptoms, both physiological and psychological. As the clinician sifts through past and present drug use, she still needs to determine if the symptoms led to drug use or the drug use led to the symptoms. Further, it is often difficult to know who has a legitimate dual diagnosis (substance use and a mental health disorder) and who is experiencing symptoms of the other disorder (whether it is the mental illness or the substance use) simply as a result of the other. The bottom line with co-occurring illnesses is that what matters most is helping the person feel understood and letting him know there is help. In our experience, many people present to treatment who could have both a mental health and a substance use problem. It is also our experience that sometimes one diagnosis dissipates as the other is treated. With people who have a primary diagnosis of substance use disorder, the mental health issues often become much more manageable.

This chapter will serve only as an introduction to working with someone who, besides having an addiction, has a notable mental illness diagnosis. It was estimated in 2014 that nearly eight million Americans who have a substance use disorder also have a co-occurring illness that could be treated as well (SAMHSA, 2014). These most often include some type of anxiety or mood disorder. There are many types of anxiety disorders, including generalized anxiety and obsessive-compulsive disorder, and even phobias are considered anxiety disorders, although the significance here of phobias is minimal. In our experience, the most common co-occurring anxiety disorder is generalized anxiety disorder. Mood disorders include depression, dysthymia, and the bipolar (formally called manic-depressive) disorders.

Bipolar disorder is a common diagnosis that might lead to substance use. Generally, people with bipolar disorder enjoy the high of the mania and sometimes use substances to achieve it. Cocaine would be a drug that brings about mania. On other occasions, the individual suffering with bipolar disorder might use sedatives or alcohol to bring down his manic state and make it more manageable.

Depression is another diagnosis given to those with a substance use issue. The diagnosis of depression is more than just feeling depressed; it is a cluster of individual symptoms that together meet the criteria for depression. One of the biggest concerns with both depression and the bipolar disorders is the risk of suicide. When one has two disorders that combine the risk, there must be real concern. We will go into more detail about the anxiety and mood disorders after addressing other co-occurring illnesses.

Schizophrenia

Schizophrenia is a chronic mental health disorder that involves a disruption of reality for the individual through delusions and/or hallucinations. There can be difficulty when it comes to diagnosing schizophrenia that co-occurs with substance use. The individual may appear psychotic under the influence of drugs or in some cases while in withdrawal, but if psychosis persists past the substance use, a psychotic disorder (including the likelihood of schizophrenia) is generally the diagnosis.

Because of the dual diagnosis, the course of action is to treat both simultaneously and with caution. The schizophrenia should first be addressed through psychopharmacotherapy, given that if the drug or alcohol is taken away, the individual will adversely react to experiencing psychotic symptoms (Starr, Bermak, Mao, Rodriguez, & Alphs, 2018). Moreover, because drug and alcohol use can and will exacerbate psychotic symptoms, interfere with medications to control the symptomatology, and increase the risk of serious medical complications, including death, it is important to get the person to discontinue his or her use.

Alcohol is the most commonly abused substance by those with schizophrenia. It is speculated that much of the high rate of alcohol use and addiction stems from the need to self-medicate in order to alleviate the symptoms of schizophrenia (Frances et al.,

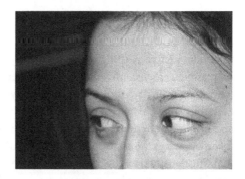

FIGURE 12.1. Those with disorders that contribute to paranoia, delusions, or hallucinations do not respond well to typical confrontational substance abuse treatment.

2005). Once the person is stable, whether this is through hospitalization (which is often necessary) or through other means, including medication management, the alcohol issues can readily be addressed.

It is important to recognize when working with someone with a psychotic disorder that his needs are similar to all other people; he wants to belong and he wants something of interest in his life. Fear of ridicule and rejection may play a part in keeping him isolated, so therapeutic work should focus on finding positive ways to meet these needs. There is often a tendency to stay only with family members and not venture out to meet others. Socialization skills can be introduced and then modeled in group settings.

Justin, a 32-year-old Caucasian male, had long been diagnosed with schizophrenia and was now in treatment for his alcohol abuse. For over a year, he used no alcohol and was on medication management. In doing so, he stayed in his house and interacted only with his mother. As a thirty-something-year-old man, this became very boring. In group sessions he would claim this was fine, and discussions of alternative activities were met with resistance. Justin eventually became frustrated with his situation and began leaving the home to walk around in the city. He felt very uncomfortable interacting with "normal" people. He eventually came across a group of individuals who would gather at the park around dusk to drink. It isn't hard to imagine that he eventually returned to alcohol use. Lack of stimulation at home and wanting to fit in combined to trigger this relapse.

Another aspect in treating those with psychotic disorders is the necessity to move away from the typically confrontational stance that substance use treatment generally utilizes. Those with a psychotic disorder do not fare well in treatment when confrontation is the general modality. The stress of confrontation can be overwhelming to a completely stable individual; confrontation is even more of a risk with someone suffering with schizophrenia. A supportive and mildly challenging stance must be taken with those suffering with this disorder. Before we transition into personality disorders, we want to put forth that Cluster A personality disorders are very similar to psychotic disorders and should also be treated with compassion and as little confrontation as possible. These personality disorders include the paranoid, schizoid, and schizotypal personality disorders. You can tell by the taxonomy alone that they are similar to the schizophrenic disorders. One of the most important—and hardest things to do in therapy with someone with any of these psychotic disorders or the personality disorders is to build trust. This is difficult, as people with these disorders tend to be very distrustful.

Personality Disorders

Personality disorders are common in people who use substances, and as with all diagnoses, it is often difficult to determine if there is a legitimate personality disorder or if the substance use simply makes it seem that way. It is important for the therapist to understand what defines a personality disorder. The most common personality disorders with a co-occurring addiction are Cluster B personality disorders (Straussner, 2014) They include the dramatic, erratic, and emotional behaviors. They are the narcissistic, borderline, histrionic, and anti-social personality disorders. It is important to note that antisocial personality disorder does not reflect someone who remains isolated or is afraid to socialize (those symptoms might be part of the symptomatology of a person with an anxiety disorder) but someone who has no regard for social rules. They are lawbreakers, and the most abundant population of this disorder is found in prisons (although there is also a high population of substance users in prison).

Most people, when in active addiction, would be perceived as having antisocial personality disorder. Many addicted individuals lie, manipulate, and only care about themselves. For many who are addicted, no rule seems worthy of abiding. For many, however, this illegal and antisocial behavior ceases shortly after abstinence from substances. In these cases, the antisocial behavior was largely due to substance use.

In treating addicts, there is often what appears to be a co-occurring mental issue. Often this diagnosis is accurate, and not only for the time of the addiction.

There are times the addiction clears up with abstinence and some behavioral changes are needed to treat the co-occurring disorder. We have seen many a male client who appeared to have antisocial personality disorder remain abstinent and become productive and law-abiding members of society.

One of the personality disorders most commonly diagnosed among addicts is borderline personality disorder (Trull et al., 2018). **Borderline personality disorder** is characterized by mood swings, relationships that seem extremely close but then become distant (often described as I love you/hate you) and self-destructive behavior that can include poor impulse control, drug use, and suicidal gestures that are often superficial. We have seen many clients who received this diagnosis but whose symptoms cleared up following abstinence. We avoid using this diagnosis because of its overrepresentation in women unless these types of behaviors continue despite abstinence from substances.

It is sometimes most difficult to determine if an individual using substances also has a personality disorder from this cluster. However, the symptoms must be treated whether or not they originate from substances or a deeper-lying problem. Once abstinence is obtained, an individual with a personality disorder would need to continue in therapy long term to help address these deep-rooted issues.

The final cluster of personality disorders is Cluster C, and includes obsessive-compulsive personality disorder and dependent and avoidant personality disorders. As these personality disorders are of the anxious type, the recommendations for working with those with anxiety disorders also apply. One important consideration in treating this cluster is that it often goes undiagnosed, as the symptoms reflect those of an addiction, including dependency issues, compulsive behaviors, and insecurity. If someone has the personality disorder as well as the addiction, he may progress more slowly than expected.

Depression

It has often been said to clients entering treatment who were concerned they might have depression, "With the shape your life is in, who wouldn't be depressed?" This statement is not to minimize their feelings, but to both normalize the feelings and allay some of their fears that they will have a lifelong illness to contend with besides addiction.

Many people feel depression is a side effect of the addiction and the havoc it wreaks in people's lives (Beaufort, et al., 2017). Others feel that the depressed individual is simply self-medicating to cope with his hopeless feelings. One undeniable fact is that people with depression are approximately two times more likely to have an alcohol addiction diagnosis (Namratha & Yeedulapally, 2018).

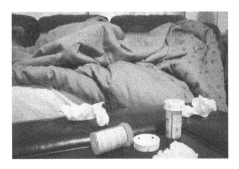

FIGURE 12.2. Depression can lead to self-medication with substances, which might result in an addiction. Additionally, it complicates addiction treatment and substantially increases the risk of suicide.

Unfortunately, occasionally dual diagnosis goes unnoticed, and mental health symptoms are simply attributed to the addiction. Many who sought treatment for addiction in the 1980s may have had a mental health diagnosis that remained undiagnosed (Foundations Recovery Network, 2018). At the same time, mental health therapists might miss the fact that a depressed client they are treating also has a substance use problem. This is especially true when the client minimizes his use (as most would, and as covered in earlier chapters along with other distortions of thinking). The important thing for those working with clients in early recovery is to continue to monitor their thought processes and be aware there may be another issue that needs to be addressed.

Maria, a 44-year-old Cuban female, identifies as a recovering alcoholic. She gave up drinking last month. Prior to last month, she reported drinking since the age of 14. Her drinking became excessive in her mid-30s (she couldn't remember exactly when). Up until last month, Maria was drinking almost a bottle (700 mL) of vodka per day. Two weeks ago, Maria was discharged from a detox center. She is staying at a family member's home and has support to help her refrain from drinking. Maria is starting to feel the "itch." She feels sad, lacks motivation, feels hopeless and helpless. Maria feels like she has no desire to live. All she can think about is drinking to avoid experiencing this pain. She is starting to recall that she had these feelings, this intensely, when she was younger. She discovered that she began drinking more significantly to "numb out" the pain of the sadness. Maria has co-occurring depression and alcohol dependence.

This is one reason continued therapy can be of great benefit. One important thing for clinicians to be aware of is that people with addictions often distort the truth to protect the coping mechanism they have come to rely on: substances.

Anxiety Disorders

Among the most common mental health disorders are anxiety disorders. Although many anxiety disorder sufferers do not engage in treatment (phobias are common but rarely treated), in our experience the most common anxiety disorder associated with addiction treatment is generalized anxiety disorder. Second to this is the social anxiety that many people who abuse drugs experience.

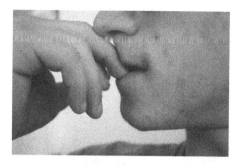

FIGURE 12.3. The most common forms of mental health disorders are those from the category of anxiety disorders.

Everyone experiences anxiety; it is a normal part of the human experience. People with an anxiety disorder experience it more often and more intensely. It is also common in some situations, like parties, for alcohol to be present. As a result, someone with anxiety might learn that alcohol, and possibly other drugs, helps quell the nervousness. This is often reinforced, and the person may come to rely on substances to reduce his anxiety in these situations.

Additionally, certain prescription drugs for anxiety do an excellent job of reducing the anxiety but lead to both physical and psychological addiction (Beaufort, et al., 2017). We have treated quite a few patients over the years who became addicted to their antianxiety medicine. It was very difficult for them to initially to get off the medication, but once they did, they often wondered what they were doing on it at all. They felt much better after a period free of benzodiazepines and on a medication less addictive.

The main issue with anxiety disorders and substance use is the overdependence on substances to quell the anxiety. Alcohol or other sedatives reduce anxiety, and then the person may come to rely on them. The thought of giving them up can be daunting. The actual withdrawal and post-acute withdrawal can make the task feel nearly impossible.

Summary

There is much that can be written about the treatment of dual disorders. This chapter introduced the reader to several of the most common diagnoses accompanying the diagnosis of addiction. Although it is not a comprehensive text about treating dual disorders, it is instead an introduction to some of the complications and what can be expected. The disorders introduced in the chapter included schizophrenia and the Cluster A personality disorders, which require an even more patient and nonconfrontational approach than usually prescribed for those dually diagnosed; anxiety disorders and the related Cluster C personality disorders; mood disorders, including depression and bipolar disorder and their increased risk of suicidality; and Cluster B personality disorders, which are the most commonly found personality disorders in addiction treatment.

Treating dual disorders is difficult and can complicate the treatment process. One provider with a working knowledge of mental health disorders and addiction treatment is certainly more effective than a client receiving treatment from two different providers. The most important aspect of treating a person with more than one diagnosis is a patient, tolerant, and respectful approach. However, if one is not knowledgeable and comfortable treating those with dual disorders, a referral is in order.

Key Terms

Dual diagnosis

Schizophrenia

Personality disorder

Borderline personality disorder

CHAPTER THIRTEEN

Harm Reduction

Learning Objectives

- Understand the nature of controlled use.
- Define medical marijuana and its use.
- Identify the concept of maintenance.
- Understand the purpose of opioid agonist therapy.
- Define methadone and methadone maintenance.
- Understand suboxone and the access of suboxone clinics.

Introduction

In the field of addiction, the choices of treatment fall under the umbrella of either abstinence or harm reduction. Most people would define recovery with abstinence; yet, harm reduction is an essential piece to the healing process. The nature of harm reduction is controlled use. Individuals, with their treatment facilitator, identify a goal of abstinence and titrate toward that goal from their current level of use. Once an acceptable, tolerable, and healthier level of use is obtained, the counselor will provide support for the maintenance of that level. If abstinence is not the goal of treatment, maintenance is then the measure of success. This would suggest that the individual has developed motivation to hold their use at a level that allows them clarity of mind and the ability to follow through with daily responsibilities. Subsequent to the maintenance stage, the counselor's role is one which provides additional motivation, and, in some cases, monitoring. The success of harm reduction strategies has gained notice by public officials around the globe. Many governments are instituting harm reduction treatment options to mitigate their substance abuse epidemic

(Hawk, Vaca, & D'Onofrio, 2015). This alone boasts its merit and efficacy as a more realistic approach to treatment.

> In a particular harm reduction group, all members were younger than 25 years old. Three of the five members had decided to cease their drug of choice (an opioid) but continued using other substances. One member continued using cannabis and alcohol, the other two continued using alcohol only: one of these two individuals drinks only minimally at social engagements, the other more regularly. See their stories in the coming paragraphs.

Before proceeding with the chapter, we will first provide an explanation as to why harm reduction is the counseling of choice with these three individuals mentioned in the case example above. The most obvious reason is when a client seeks treatment; the goals are determined as a negotiation between both the client and the clinician. If the client does not have the goal of abstinence, the clinician has several choices: Refer the client to a facility that will work with him in either an abstinence or harm reduction fashion; highlight the benefits of abstinence; or work with him with harm reduction as the goal. This does not always mean simply accepting that the client will use. Fundamentally, **harm reduction** is intended to reduce the negative consequences and high-risk behaviors associated with drug abuse. Let's use the group discussed above as an example. It is important to note that all members in the group sought treatment for opioid addiction (prescription pain killers). Some also used other substances, but opioids were the drug of choice.

FIGURE 13.1. Harm reduction treatment is considered the third wave of addiction treatment, challenging the abstinence-only model.

There is the client who drinks minimally and occasionally. He sought treatment as a result of addiction to opioids and has remained abstinent from them for over a year. In his history, he also used marijuana consistently and may have had an addiction to it before using opioids. Currently, he drinks minimally and occasionally. Initially, his drinking was monitored closely, and he never had more than a beer or two with a meal. Recently he reported he drank six beers over the course of as many hours while tailgating at a college game. The individual does not demonstrate a great deal of addictive thinking that many clients in treatment do and certainly has not demonstrated it with alcohol while in treatment.

The second member reports realizing he would benefit from quitting drinking but has not committed to it yet (preparation stage of change). Like the others, one of his drugs was an opioid, but he also used a sedative (Xanax) regularly as well as alcohol. He had been drinking minimally at the beginning of treatment after a short period of abstinence following a brief inpatient treatment. By the end of his treatment, he was drinking excessively and had relapsed with Xanax on several occasions. He terminated treatment, feeling it was no longer necessary. This, of course, was against the recommendation of the therapist.

The third client attempting harm reduction also was addicted to opioids. He completed a 90-day inpatient treatment before coming to the group. He did not believe abstinence from all substances was for him. From the first session, he reported that although he had been abstinent to that point, he will use alcohol on his 21st birthday. He also reported being open to marijuana use. He used both alcohol and marijuana before his birthday. In fact, it was at a point where both the group and this therapist saw the progression and felt he displayed an addiction to these substances. Following the group's intervention, he agreed that to use more than two days in a week would indicate he is not in control.

Controlled Use

Controlled use is the client's goal to continue the use of a substance in a fashion that is controlled, monitored, and less debilitating. This is a commonly used approach with a less damaging or more socially accepted substance, such as marijuana or alcohol. The client usually believes complete abstinence is unnecessary or unimaginable. The client believes he has a good chance at succeeding at controlling his use and feels that the effort involved is worth it. This compassionate and pragmatic understanding of the addicted person's experience is the root of harm reduction. Originally born out of Europe, first efforts of controlled use began with needle exchange programs (Marlatt, 1996). These programs commonly offered education on the proper use of needles, as well as a safer environment for needle use. Moreover, controlled use methods can also be successful with alcohol and marijuana use. Through steady and measured support, certain individuals have been found to use a consistent and smaller amount of substances with limited negative consequences, if any at all. The abstinence-only model does not factor in cultural and age implications. For many cohorts, perhaps even generationally, mild alcohol and marijuana use is a cultural norm. A number of relapses occur because of the difficulty in resisting use in social settings. Further, implications of beneficial use have been rising, particularly with marijuana (Campbell, Twenge, & Carter, 2017). In 1996, California was the first state to legalize medical marijuana. **Medical marijuana** is the use of the whole marijuana plant or its extracts to treat medical ailments under the supervision of a healthcare provider. In this case, marijuana may be smoked or ingested by a pill or oil. As of 2018, 33 states have legalized medical marijuana. In doing so, residents receive a medical marijuana card, and their use is monitored by a healthcare provider. Many speculate that prior to this, individuals were self-medicating to manage their ailments. This legalized, controlled-use model allows for individuals to manage their substance use and symptoms accordingly with supervision.

The rewards of controlled use harm reduction therapy are apparent in these examples. The first case example in the box demonstrates that harm reduction can work for some individuals. This client may live the rest of his life without a problem with alcohol or without a relapse into his drug of choice. The focus of treatment was gaining understanding of the risks of continued substance use to the goal of remaining abstinent from his drug of choice. Additionally, the importance of not allowing the alcohol use to progress into a problem of its own was a priority of treatment. From that point, the use was monitored, and the focus of treatment was on personal growth and relational issues that may contribute to relapse or otherwise negative outcomes.

In regard to the other cases where substance use may be becoming an issue, the fact that the client remained engaged in treatment may be the of the most importance, if there is no other reward. When a clinician discharges a client from treatment for not remaining abstinent, he may be unintentionally playing into the addiction. Although the person choosing to use drugs is ultimately responsible for his behavior, the facility discharging the individual is sending the perceived message, "We are giving up on you," and that can contribute to the continuation of the addiction. So again, at worst, the reward for harm reduction is keeping the client engaged in treatment.

As a positive from this, when the client is in treatment, the group and the therapist can challenge his thinking and hopefully provide positive peer pressure toward a healthier choice. As part of this, the client will often make agreements regarding the extent of substance use. If he fails to keep to his set standards, he has to look at himself or again activate addictive-thinking defense mechanisms, which can again be challenged.

Amanda is 26 year old Hispanic American female. She was suffering from alcohol abuse and periodic marijuana use. Amanda tried abstinence three times without success. Her efforts left her feeling helpless and hopeless. A friend referred her to a harm reduction group. She was confused at first about the intention of the group but then quickly realized how "cool" it was. Amanda was excited that there was a professional who said it was okay for her to use. Amanda continued to abuse alcohol in her first week, not fully understanding the purpose of the group. She shared her behavior with the members the following week. The therapist and members offered her feedback. Amanda quickly learned that she shouldn't share. She would often tune out in group and disregard feedback from others. Eight months later, Amanda was the only remaining original member of her group. The other members achieved success and moved on. Amanda reached her breaking point. After an individual consultation, the therapist issued her a behavioral chart that quantified the amount she could drink with a decreasing momentum over the next two months. With a renewed commitment to treatment, she stuck to the behavioral chart and was able to successfully abstain. Amanda's next hurdle is to maintain sobriety, but for now, she is happy with her accomplishment.

The problem with this is the risk of enabling the continuation of the addiction, as well as the return of addictive thinking, which leaves the client unable to clearly perceive the progression of his use or otherwise justifying it. With these concerns in mind, it is important to set limits with the harm reduction client and to stick to them, providing consequences if they do not make some progress in the treatment process.

Maintenance

Maintenance refers to the use of a less harmful substance in order to reduce the chance of relapse into the drug of choice, which is causing problems. The most common example is for opioid addiction. **Opioid agonist therapy** has been the most widely recognized treatment for opioid dependence and has gained significant government support (Nadelmann & LaSalle, 2017). The aim of this type of harm reduction treatment is not just to reduce the use of opioids but also to prevent overdose. Opioid agonists are successful because they stimulate the same brain receptors without the experience of severe withdrawal and cravings. The first common drug for maintenance in the past was **methadone**, still in large use today. **Methadone maintenance** is used to substitute a longer-acting opioid (generally the longer-acting drugs stay in the system longer and produce less dramatic psychoactive effects), such as heroin or prescription pain killers. The addicted individual gets a dose of methadone daily that staves off withdrawal and also blocks the effect of another opioid (Livingston, Adams, Jordan, MacMillan, & Hering, 2018). The typical course of methadone maintenance ranges from one to several years. When engaged in methadone maintenance, it is often a requirement of the treatment center that the individual have frequent follow-ups. This serves a double purpose: the individual does not experience withdrawal and does not get the reward of other drug use. Further, methadone maintenance minimizes the rate of relapse among drug users versus no treatment at all (Wegman et al., 2017). When one considers the rate of opioid overdose deaths in the United States alone in 2017 was over 72,000, it is clear why access to opioid agonist therapy is critical. However, methadone is typically only available in treatment centers. This limits access to only those who have been lucky enough to be accepted into those centers. Gaining in popularity due to its greater access and paralleled efficacy to methadone is Suboxone (Bondar, Durigan, Haugh, & Wilson, 2018).

Suboxone binds with opioid receptors similarly to any other opioid, without stimulating the receptor (reduced effect) and while preventing withdrawal and reducing craving. This medication has grown in popularity because of its safety, efficacy, and access. **Suboxone clinics** have become significantly more pervasive that methadone treatment centers simply because of the U.S. Drug Enforcement Agency's (DEA) regulations associated with each drug classification. Methadone is a Schedule 2 drug, whereas Suboxone is a Schedule 3 drug. Schedule 2 drugs are known for their highly addictive properties, which means that when prescribed, the patient must be more frequently and closely monitored. On the other hand, Suboxone produces less euphoric effects and has fewer addictive properties. Physician's are able to prescribe Suboxone directly from their primary care office once they have their Suboxone DEA license. Therefore, a suboxone clinic could potentially be any doctor's office in your neighborhood.

With any of these medications, the goal is to cease the illicit substance use. Proponents argue maintenance reduces crime and the cost to society while allowing the addict to live a more normal life. Detractors argue that it is simply an addiction to a more acceptable substance. Both have valid arguments. We believe maintenance can be very effective when used appropriately. As with any of these types of interventions, maintenance is overutilized. We have seen and heard of young people, not even in their twenties, being put on maintenance, which is intended as a long-term treatment. Some opioid addicts spend their entire lives on maintenance. Although we believe it effective as a last-resort treatment, we believe it is often resorted to too quickly. This may be at the behest of the addict, feeling he cannot create a successful life without a substance. Other times, because it offers relief from both a painful psychological addiction and physical withdrawal, doctors are quick to prescribe it in their desire to help.

It has been generally taught, and continues to be purported by many, that you do not get high from these substances. That is not at all true, although maintenance drugs are less apt to get you high in proper doses than the opioid of choice. For example, in one particular community mental health agency there was a methadone program. Not only did some sell their methadone dose at the corner store (in this case that meant spitting the dose from the users mouth back into a container to sell, which someone then bought with full awareness of this), but also there were break-ins where methadone was the target. If a substance sells on the street, it generally has some mind- and mood-altering effect. There is no corner Prozac dealer.

More recently, the advent and more common use of buprenorphine (Subutex and Suboxone) have seen too many people "losing" their prescription, or their mother flushing it, or their dog eating it, to believe it doesn't have some effect on getting high.

Maintenance can be effective when two things are considered. First, that it is the appropriate intervention at the time (it does not have to remain lifelong, and work in therapy can be done to encourage the patient to adopt a drug-free lifestyle when appropriate), and secondly, when it is a last resort.

In a span of five years at the center mentioned above, two clients who had decided to be drug free were referred from the methadone clinic. There were hundreds of active clients in the clinic at any given time, but only two were referred, which is quite a statement. This is indicative of the status quo problem that engulfs far too many people, addicted or not. People get so used to something that it just continues on, and they forget there are other options—with no one to encourage a client further, this can be debilitating.

A type of maintenance briefly mentioned earlier in this text was marijuana maintenance. This occurs when an individual stops what is generally thought to be a harder drug and only uses marijuana. This can occur with other substances, especially alcohol, but we prefer using marijuana as the example, as it is the most likely to bring about success. Further, the legalization of medical marijuana in 33 states allows for this to occur with a more controlled process. At mentioning success, however, we'd like to make it clear we neither advocate this plan nor does it meet our definition of success. But in the treatment of individuals, it is not always the therapist's definition that is most important.

When a person puts down a substance that is creating havoc in his life, this change is an enormous one. The individual is attempting to change more than a habit—it is a lifestyle change that must occur. Using another substance in place of the drug of choice is a high-risk and low-payoff endeavor for most. First, the risk of relapse returning to the drug of choice is great. Second, the problem behavior, which is actually the need to escape painful feelings and uncomfortable situations, is not addressed. As this is a core issue with addiction, not addressing it often leads to a substitution of addictive behaviors. If one is using another substance, this risk is great. It is almost normal for those in early recovery to experience a time when they overdo other things. It might be shopping, impulsive purchases, sex, relationships, and even healthy alternatives like exercise. When someone is substituting a substance, there is a high likelihood he will overuse the other substance.

The other risk is that the person will not achieve the lifestyle change, the change in philosophy of living that can be so important and life altering. For now it is important to understand that for the ultimate recovery, it is essential to have this philosophy change. When a substance like marijuana or alcohol is substituted, this change rarely occurs.

Summary

Harm reduction can take two forms: controlled use or maintenance. Controlled use can also offer several rewards, including a more normalized life for the client, and the client remaining in treatment, where any return to substance problems or addictive thinking can be addressed. There are also drawbacks, including what might be considered enabling behavior.

Harm reduction also includes interventions such as needle exchange and opioid agonist therapy. In these treatments, the goal is providing services that result in less harm, both to the individual (such as less blood-borne disease or risk of overdose) or to society (fewer health care dollars and less crime). Harm reduction has inarguable benefits and can also lead to clients making healthier choices, including, eventually, complete abstinence, which is more in line with traditional treatment goals.

Key Terms

Harm reduction	Opioid agonist therapy	Methadone maintenance
Controlled use	Methadone	Suboxone
Medical marijuana		Suboxone clinics
Maintenance		

CHAPTER FOURTEEN

Spirituality and Recovery

Learning Objectives

- Explain why it was important to address spirituality in a textbook on addiction recovery.
- Discuss how an atheist may fare in a 12-step program.
- Describe in simple terms some of the tenets of major world religions.
- Discuss why the founders of AA felt a "spiritual cure" was appropriate.
- Identify why some people have lost faith in religion or religious teachings.
- Discuss the authors' final thoughts on addiction recovery and the struggles it entails.

Introduction

It is necessary to address the topic of spirituality directly, as it has been alluded to several times in this text. Many people who enter treatment for addiction recovery are taken aback by the spiritual concepts normally associated with a recovery program. Others initially welcome the spiritual aspects, returning to a religious belief system they once were familiar with, as it instills a sense of hope for them. Still others view the 12-step program as a cult-like movement because of the rituals and perceived necessity by its members. Others are atheists and have trouble with any program that suggests they rely upon an unseen force or entity. This section will attempt to address these circumstances, as well as provide some spiritual beliefs that the reader may have been previously unfamiliar with. It will also focus on some of the similarities between religions of the world, spirituality, and the 12-step program.

FIGURE 14.1. Spirituality is a key aspect of recovery according to mental health recovery-oriented and strengths model proponents. (Gomi, Starnino, & Canda, 2014)

Considering psychological well-being generally, many studies have been conducted addressing spirituality, meaning in life, and religiosity in relation to mental health. Studies seem to indicate that meaning in life leads to better psychological outcomes (Peres, Kamei, Tobo, & Luccetti, 2018). According to Peres and colleagues "there is a significant association between high religiousness and high meaning, highlighting the role of religion in the search for meaning and peace." Simply, religion provides meaning, and meaning contributes to better mental health outcomes. Despite the effect of religiosity on finding meaning, even atheists and agnostics who find meaning in life have better outcomes.

With that said, we will begin by addressing the atheist entering recovery, as this is the easiest to address in relation to spirituality and recovery.

An **atheist** is someone who denies the existence of any higher power. In this case, in regard to typical 12-step-based treatment, the only suggestion we have is to make the group conscience of the 12-step meeting your higher power. The recovering person can bounce his decisions off of a few other people, including recovering people, and follow the consensus. The 12-step programs have an excellent acronym for GOD: **Good Orderly Direction**. If a consensus of recovering people lean toward a certain decision, and the client has been honest with them (not manipulated the facts to guide others toward the decision he or she wants to make), then this is good orderly direction. It is beneficial to use recovering people or people who have a thorough understanding of recovery for advice and feedback because they are aware of more of the intricacies of recovery and its effect on thinking. After all, any good addict could probably get a group of people who know little about recovery to condone his drinking beer or wine or smoking marijuana, especially if these were not the drugs of choice.

An atheist generally will not bode well in a 12-step program. There are Alcoholics Anonymous meetings for atheists, but they are rare, and they generally use the same 12 steps. With the overtones of spirituality in the 12-step movement, an atheist would likely never involve himself in such a program. However, since a spiritual solution to addiction is an effective one for many people, we hope that an open mind in the atheist will prevail. There are alternative support groups, as discussed in Chapter 5. An atheist or agnostic could try SMART Recovery, which is based on cognitive therapy techniques, or

Refuge Recovery, which though Buddhist in nature, does not require a spiritual acceptance beyond one's experience.

This discussion will be largely spiritual in nature, and it is our hope the atheist will not simply stop reading here (if he has made it this far). As for **agnostics** (those who are unsure whether a higher power exists), we do not believe we can say it any better than the authors did in the "We Agnostics" chapter of the Alcoholics Anonymous' *Big Book* (Alcoholics Anonymous, 2001). We recommend the agnostic reader go there.

To any individual who has difficulty accepting the tenets of his given religion, we encourage exploration. When faced with adversity (like recovery from drug addiction), many people return with fervor to a religion they knew from earlier days. Some, however, have an aversion to any religion. We have seen many people faced with addiction recovery who have an aversion to religion explore other spiritual and philosophical beliefs. It has long been our contention that a change in philosophy must occur to maintain abstinence. We refer the reader to chapter 4, "The Cognitive Processes Involved in Addiction," where we initially discussed how a change in philosophy is the end result of challenging thinking. In addition, changing one's philosophy can make challenging thinking more effective. This makes exploring different philosophies and spiritual beliefs all the more important for those who aren't comfortable with established belief systems they are familiar with.

There are many world religions, and there would be no way we could include them all here. We will address some of the major ones and present a minimal overview of their core beliefs.

World Religions

What follows is a very brief and certainly not exhaustive review of some of the major world religions. This is provided in an attempt to eliminate misconceptions about religions that may be unfamiliar to the reader. When working with those in substance use treatment, it is essential that the clients understand other belief systems if they are to enter a 12-step program. It is the experience of many therapists that at times clients are unaware of other religious beliefs. In some religions, simply believing differently goes against the tenets of the religion and would be perceived as sinful and possibly demonic.

Judaism—Includes different interpretations of the sacred text as with most major religions. The best explanation of the Jewish God, for those familiar with the bible, is the God from the Old Testament. There are guidelines for behavior and for entrance to heaven. There is no threat of hell. There has not yet been a messiah or savior.

Christianity—This religion includes many different **sects**: Catholic, Protestant, Baptist, Jehovah's Witnesses, for example. Christianity purports that Jesus Christ is the savior, and He must be accepted as such to reach heaven. Failure to do so results in condemnation to hell or nonexistence. The rules surrounding other aspects of Christianity vary by sect.

Islam—This religion also has sects. The God of Islam, usually referred to as Allah, is similar to the God of the Jewish and Christian religions in that He will render judgment. A core belief is that Muhammad was a prophet after the time of Jesus (who was a prophet, not the savior). Islam's holy book is the *Qur'an* (Koran).

Buddhism—Another religion with varying sects. The goal is enlightenment; there is no afterlife, as Westerners understand it. Some sects believe in reincarnation, others believe in a simple return to energy, which permeates all living things. The Buddha is not God, and there are actually several Buddhas. A Buddha is anyone who attains nirvana and returns to this existence until all living things are enlightened.

Hinduism—Again, there are varying sects. Believers of this religion believe in one God who is at once everything and more than everything. Everything that makes up this reality is God, or Brahman, as it is called in the Hindu religion. Reincarnation as another living being is a central belief.

Taoism—Taoism is an Eastern natural religion, also with differing beliefs by varying sects. Generally speaking, the higher power is a force that moves through all. When working in flow with this force, things are good; when acts go against the flow, things are harder. There is no judgment, just being in or out of the flow.

Of course, there are many other religions that have not been covered, but these are the world's major religions. One interesting aspect about the world religions is how people argue about which is right and look at religions other than their own with fear or disdain, and yet these religions are so similar. All religions have guidelines for behavior, for which the ultimate goal is to bring one closer to their higher power. For example, in the Jewish and Christian religions, there are commandments that guide one's behavior. The Islamic religion also has commandments that guide one's behavior for the benefit of all humanity. In Buddhism, there is the Eightfold Path to enlightenment, which consists of guidelines such as right intention, right action, and right speech, among others. In the Hindu religion, all living things are part of "God," thereby implying that one would act accordingly and do no harm. It seems a reasonable assumption, then, that all religions impress upon their followers to behave in a fashion that most rational people would perceive as good.

Religion and the 12 Steps

Someone who is familiar with the 12 steps of any 12-step program (as they are all similar, with some semantic changes to address the particular malady) would likely agree that the 12-step program is also a guideline for behavior that will bring one closer to a higher power. Bill Wilson, a cofounder of Alcoholics Anonymous, at times corresponded with Carl Jung, a prominent psychiatrist and psychoanalyst of the time. In a letter Jung wrote to Wilson, he described alcoholism as a "thirst for wholeness." This is interpreted as a longing to be closer to one's God. Carl Jung, and then Bill Wilson, held a belief that alcoholism required a spiritual cure. Wilson prescribed the cure in the 12 steps.

If we step back for a moment, it is easy to see why the 12-step programs are considered spiritual programs. There is room for any religious belief, any higher power, but a belief in something beyond the realm of perceived reality is helpful.

We would like to step back even further. At the risk of offending anyone, we propose that all religions share guidelines to enlightened living. Perhaps rather than just one religion being right, they all are different paths to the same goal. And perhaps this goal—enlightened living and the proper treatment of all living things—is the goal of all of humanity and the only goal any God wants.

Harry, a 42-year-old Caucasian male who is a nonpracticing Catholic, has just entered AA. Looking through the literature, he is deterred by the mention of "God." Harry left the Catholic church because he no longer agreed with the dogma of the institution and avoided any person or group that "forced" God on him. Harry expressed his concerns to other members and heard them explain that it is more about spirituality than a "religion." Despite his disbelief, Harry continued to attend meetings over the next month. After making progress with the steps, Harry saw the 12 steps as guidelines and that he actually created his own experience in the meetings. He created his own meaning. Harry, to this day, is a strong advocate of 12-step meetings. He still does not identify as Catholic, but is happy to identify as a recovering alcoholic.

Regardless of whether our proposition that religions are a path to the same goal is correct or not, the benefit of the 12 steps to a recovering individual is undeniable. Most people in recovery who have worked the 12 steps will readily agree the program has had a spiritual effect on them. This is not to say that they are beyond reproach. Many 12-step members, as well as Christians, Muslims, Buddhists, or Hindus, fall short at times of the beliefs they purport. All humans fall short. This is, at times, difficult to take, especially for someone new to recovery who has perfectionist ideals. It is also a reason many lose faith, whether it is in the 12-step program or in their religion. We mention this so when any client witnesses someone fall short of his stated or implied beliefs and discusses this with his counselor, the counselor explores whether he is using it as a rationalization to abandon a spiritual program.

The 12 steps promise a spiritual awakening as a result of following them. There are, however, pitfalls or roadblocks for many along the way. In this world we live in, it is often difficult to keep a spiritual focus, especially when dealing with the daily problems that arise in life. Perhaps betrayal by a person who projects a religious image has resulted in a loss of faith. Or perhaps a client is tempted to denounce all who follow a spiritual purpose as deluded. Perhaps the recovering person feels God has let him or her down in the past. Or perhaps just negative experiences with religious zealots make one fear becoming one. Whatever the obstacles or roadblocks, the therapist can help by exploring these obstacles, helping the client challenge distorted thinking, and assisting him in finding and/or defining his beliefs.

Summary

Many who recover from addiction take a spiritual path or utilize a spiritual component to assist in their remission from substances. Some individuals with substance use problems have had extremely negative experiences in their religion and may benefit from exploration of other beliefs, and some return to their religion with fervor.

Twelve-step programs have a strong spiritual component, which many of your clients will be confronted with. As such, discussion of spiritual aspects becomes essential to working with those who have substance use issues. This chapter introduces the reader to some of the tenets of different religions and encourages an understanding of this for one's clients as well.

In conclusion, we hope we have addressed some of the spiritual aspects of the recovery process. We believe it is essential in recovery to work a program of personal growth that enhances the self and relationships with others. The steps are a simple program that lays out a formula for personal growth and spiritual awakening. It has been proven to work in the lives of many an alcoholic and addict. Beyond being sober, a new life emerges, one with new perspectives, hopefully a sense of purpose, and a connection with a higher power.

Many scholars believe that the door to enlightenment is first opened through suffering. It is our opinion that suffering can serve a purpose. Often, with distance between you and difficult times, insight reveals the benefits of the struggles and carves the path to self-discovery, change, and eventually enlightenment.

We would like you to think about this and consider what your client's addiction and recovery, or any trial or tribulation he has experienced, might mean later in life.

Key Terms

Atheist

Good Orderly Direction

Agnostic

Judaism

Christianity

Islam

Buddhism

Hinduism

Taoism

Sects

References

Alcoholics Anonymous. (2001). We agnostics. In *Big Book* (4th ed., p. 24). New York, NY: AA World Services.

Alcoholics Anonymous. (1981). *Twelve steps and twelve traditions.* New York, NY: Alcoholics Anonymous World Services.

Alcoholics Anonymous World Services. (2012). 2014 Membership Survey. Retrieved from https://www.aa.org/assets/en_US/p-48_membershipsurvey.pdf

Alcoholics Anonymous World Services. (2018). AA around the world. Retrieved from https://www.aa.org/pages/en_US/aa-around-the-world

American Psychiatric Association. (2000). *Diagnostic and statistical manual of mental disorders* (4th ed., text rev.). Washington, DC: Author.

American Psychiatric Association. (2013). *Diagnostic and statistical manual of mental disorders* (5th ed). Washington, DC: Author.

Baldwin, J. M., Stogner, J. M., & Miller, B. L. (2014). It's five o'clock somewhere: An examination of the association between happy hour drinking and negative consequences. *Substance Abuse Treatment Prevention and Policy, 9*(17).

Banducci, A. N., Hoffman, E. M., Lejuez, C. W., & Koenen, K. C. (2014). The impact of childhood abuse on inpatient substance users: Specific links with risky sex, aggression, and emotion dysregulation. *Child Abuse & Neglect, 38*(5), 928–938.

Barbor, T. F., Biddle-Higgins, J. C., Saunders, J. B., & Monteiro, M. G. (2001). *The alcohol use disorders identification test: Guidelines for use in primary health care.* Geneva, Switzerland: World Health Organization.

Berghmans, R., de Jong, J., Tibben, A., & de Wert, G. (2009). On the biomedicalization of alcoholism. *Theoretical Medicine and Bioethics, 30*(4), 311–321. http://doi.org/10.1007/s11017-009-9103-7

Bergner, R. M. (2002). Sexual compulsion as attempted recovery from degradation: Theory and therapy. *Journal of Sex & Marital Therapy, 28*(5), 373–387.

Berry, W. (2015, June 27). The second Noble Truth: Acceptance: It isn't what you think [Web post]. Retrieved from https://www.psychologytoday.com/us/blog/the-second-noble-truth/201506/acceptance-it-isnt-what-you-think

Berry, W. (2017). The second Noble Truth: Mindfulness and acceptance in Alcoholics Anonymous [Web post]. Retrieved from https://www.psychologytoday.com/us/blog/the-second-noble-truth/201701/mindfulness-and-acceptance-in-alcoholics-anonymous

Beaufort, I. N., De Weert-Van Oene, G. H., Buwalda, V. A., de Leeuw, J. R. J., & Goudriaan, A. E. (2017). The Depression, Anxiety and Stress Scale (DASS-21) as a Screener for Depression in Substance Use Disorder Inpatients: A Pilot Study. *European addiction research*, *23*(5), 260–268.

Bian, M., & Leung, L. (2015). Linking loneliness, shyness, smartphone addiction symptoms, and patterns of smartphone use to social capital. *Social Science Computer Review*, *33*(1), 61–79.

Bommersbach, T., Lapid, A., Rummans, T., & Morse, R. (2015). Geriatric alcohol use disorder: A review for primary care physicians. *Mayo Clinic Proceedings*, *90*(5), 659–666.

Bondar, A., Durigan, C. R., Haugh, A., & Wilson, S. A. (2018). In patients with substance abuse disorder, is Suboxone® more effective than methadone for treatment of opioid dependence? *Evidence-Based Practice*, *21*(2), E3–E4.

Bowen, S., Witkiewitz, K., Clifasefi, S. L., Grow, J., Chawla, N., Hsu, S. H., … Larimer, M. E. (2014). Relative efficacy of mindfulness-based relapse prevention, standard relapse prevention, and treatment as usual for substance use disorders: A randomized clinical trial. *JAMA Psychiatry*, *71*(5), 547–556.

Briken, P., Habermann, N., Berner, W., & Hill, A. (2007). Diagnosis and treatment of sexual addiction: A survey among German sex therapists. *Sexual Addiction & Compulsivity*, *14*, 131–143.

Buckner, J. D., Heimberg, R. G., Ecker, A. H., & Vinci, C. (2013). A biopsychosocial model of social anxiety and substance use. *Depression and Anxiety*, *30*(3), 276–284.

Bunton, R., Baldwin, S., Flynn, D., & Whitelaw, S. (2000). The 'stages of change' model in health promotion: Science and ideology. *Critical Public Health*, *10*(1), 55–70.

Cacciola, J. S., Alterman, A. I., DePhilippis, D., Drapkin, M. L., Valadez, C., Fala, N. C., … McKay, J. R. (2013). Development and initial evaluation of the brief addiction monitor (BAM). *Journal of Substance Abuse Treatment*, *44*(3), 256–263.

Campbell, W., Twenge, J., & Carter, N. (2017). Support for marijuana (cannabis) legalization: Untangling age, period, and cohort effects. *Collabra: Psychology*, *3*(1).

Cannizzaro, D., Stohl, M., Hasin, D., & Aharonovich, E. (2017). Intrinsic and extrinsic motivation predict treatment outcome in sample of HIV+ drug users. *Drug and Alcohol Dependence*, *171*(e34).

Carnes, P. (1983). *Out of the shadows: Understanding sexual addiction* (3rd ed.). Center City, MN: Hazelden.

Carnes, P., Green, B., & Carnes, S. (2010) The same yet different: Refocusing the sexual addiction screening test (SAST) to reflect orientation and gender. *Sexual Addiction & Compulsivity, 17*(1), 7–30.

Celebrate Recovery. (2018). History of Celebrate Recovery. Retrieved from https://www.celebraterecovery.com/about/history-of-cr

Center of Excellence in Substance Abuse Treatment and Education. (2010). Treatment planning with brief addiction monitor (BAM). Retrieved from https://vaww.portal.va.gov/sites/OMHS/SUD/Lists/BAM/AllItems.aspx

Cox, G. B., Brown L., Hansten, M., & Morgan, C. (2001). NW HIDTA/DASA Washington State Drug Court Evaluation Project: Final Report (ADAI Technical Report 01-01). Retrieved from University of Washington, Alcohol & Drug Abuse Institute website: http://adai.washington.edu/pubs/drugcourt/fullreport.pdf

Curtis, O. (1999). *Chemical dependency: A family affair.* Belmont, CA: Brooks/Cole.

da Veiga, G. F., Sotero, L., Pontes, H. M., Cunha, D., Portugal, A., & Relvas, A. P. (2018). Emerging adults and Facebook use: The validation of the Bergen Facebook Addiction Scale (BFAS). *International Journal of Mental Health and Addiction*, 1–16. doi.org/10.1007/s11469-018-0018-2

Davis, R. A. (2001). A cognitive-behavioral model for pathological Internet use (PIU). *Computers in Human Behavior, 17*(2), 187–195.

DiClemente, C. C., Bellino, L. E., & Neavins, T. M. (1999). Motivation for change and alcoholism treatment. *Alcohol Research & Health, 23*(2), 86–86.

Dixon, M. R., Wilson, A. N., & Habib, R. (2016). Neurological evidence of acceptance and commitment therapy effectiveness in college-age gamblers. *Journal of Contextual Behavioral Science, 5*(2), 80–88.

Dobson, K. S. (2010). *Handbook of cognitive-behavioral therapies* (3rd. ed.). New York, NY: Guildford Press.

Dobson, D., & Dobson, K. S. (2017). *Evidence-based practice of cognitive therapy* (2nd. ed.). New York, NY: Guilford Press.

Dodes, L. (2002). *The heart of addiction.* New York, NY: Harper Collins.

Easwaran, E. (2010). *Conquest of mind.* Tomales, CA: Blue Mountain Center of Meditation/Nilgiri Press.

Eckberg, D. A., & Jones, D. S. (2015). "I'll just do my time": The role of motivation in the rejection of the DWI court model. *Qualitative Report, 20*(1), 130–147.

Farabee, D., Prendergast, M., & Anglin, M. D. (1998). The effectiveness of coerced treatment for drug-abusing offenders. *Fed. Probation, 62*, 3.

Fisher, G. L., & Harrison, T. C. (2009). *Substance abuse: Information for school counselors, social workers, therapists, and counselors.* Boston, MA: Pearson.

Frances, R. J., Miller, S. I., & Mack, A. H. (2005). *Clinical textbook of addictive disorders* (3rd ed.). New York, NY: Guilford Press.

Frone, M. R. (2016). Work stress and alcohol use: Developing and testing a biphasic self-medication model. *Work and Stress, 30*(4), 374–394.

Gallagher, J. R., & Bremer, T. (2018). A perspective from the field: The disconnect between abstinence-based programs and the use of motivational interviewing in treating substance use disorders. *Alcoholism Treatment Quarterly, 36*(1), 115–126.

Gomi, S., Starnino, V., & Canda, E. (2014). Spiritual Assessment in Mental Health Recovery. *Community Mental Health Journal, 50*(4), 447–453. doi:10.1007/s10597-013-9653-z

Gorski, T. T., & Miller, M. (1986). *Staying sober*. Independence, MO: Herald House/ Independence Press.

Griffiths, M. (2000). Internet addiction: Time to be taken seriously? *Addiction Research, 8*(5), 413–418.

Hall, A. S., & Parsons, J. (2001). Internet addiction: College student case study using best practices in cognitive behavior therapy. *Journal of Mental Health Counseling, 23*(4), 312–327.

Hamburg, H., & Pronk, T. (2015). Believe you can and you will: The belief in high self-control decreases interest in attractive alternatives. *Journal of Experimental Social Psychology, 56*, 30–35.

Harding, K. J. K., Rush, A. J., Arbuckle, M., Trivedi, M. H., & Pincus, H. A. (2011). Measurement-based care in psychiatric practice: A policy framework for implementation. *Journal of Clinical Psychiatry, 72*(8), 1136–1143.

Hawi, N. S., Samaha, M., & Griffiths, M. D. (2018). Internet gaming disorder in Lebanon:

Relationships with age, sleep habits, and academic achievement. *Journal of behavioral addictions, 7*(1), 70–78.

Hawk, K. F., Vaca, F. E., & D'Onofrio, G. (2015). Reducing fatal opioid overdose: Prevention, treatment and harm reduction strategies. *Yale Journal of Biology and Medicine, 88*(3), 235.

Helgoe, R. S. (2002). *The hierarchy of recovery*. Center City, MN: Hazelden.

Hook, J. N., Hook, J. P., & Hines, S. (2008). Reach out or act out: Long-term group therapy for sexual addiction. *Sexual Addiction & Compulsivity, 15*, 217–232.

Iarussi, M. M., Tyler, J. M., Crawford, S. H., & Crawford, C. V. (2016). Counselor training in two evidence-based practices: Motivational interviewing and cognitive behavioral therapy. *Journal of Counseling Preparation and Supervision, 8*(3). http://dx.doi.org/10.7729/83.1113

Jacob, K. S. (2015). Recovery model of mental illness: A complementary approach to psychiatric care. *Indian Journal of Psychological Medicine, 37*(2), 117–119.

Job, V., Walton, G. M., Bernecker, K., & Dweck, C. S. (2013). Beliefs about willpower determine the impact of glucose on self-control. *Proceedings of the National Academy of Sciences, 110*(37), 14837–14842.

Johnston, L. D., Miech, R. A., O'Malley, P. M., Bachman, J. G., Schulenberg, J. E., & Patrick, M. E. (2018). *Monitoring the Future national survey results on drug use: 1975–2017: Overview, key findings on adolescent drug use.* Retrieved from University of Michigan, Institute for Social Research website: http://www .monitoringthefuture.org/pubs/monographs/mtf-overview2017.pdf

Jones, J. M. (2018). Most in U.S. Say Consuming Alcohol, Marijuana Morally OK. *Drugs and Alcohol | Gallup Topic*, Gallup, Inc., news.gallup.com/topic/ category_drugs_and_alcohol.aspx.

Kabat-Zinn, J. (2005). *Coming to our senses: Healing ourselves and the world through mindfulness.* New York, NY: Hyperion.

Kahl, K., Winter, L., & Schweiger, U. (2012). The third wave of cognitive behavioural therapies: What is new and what is effective? *Current Opinion in Psychiatry, 25*(6), 522–52.

Kelly, J. F. (2017). Is Alcoholics Anonymous religious, spiritual, neither? Findings from 25 years of mechanisms of behavior change research. *Addiction, 112*(6), 929–936.

Kemp, S. (2018, January 30). Global digital report 2018 [Web post]. Retrieved from https://wearesocial.com/blog/2018/01/global-digital-report-2018

Kerr, J. S. (1996). Two myths of addiction: The addictive personality and the issue of free choice. *Human Psychopharmacology, 11*, S9–S13.

Kohut, H. (1971). The Analysis of the Self New York: Int.

Krystal, H., & Raskin, H. (1970). *Drug dependence: Aspects of ego function.* Detroit, MI: Wayne State University Press.

Kübler-Ross, E. 2005. *On grief and grieving: Finding the meaning of grief through the five stages of loss.* New York, NY: Simon & Schuster.

Kushnir, V., Godinho, A., Hodgins, D. C., Hendershot, C. S., & Cunningham, J. A. (2016) Motivation to quit or reduce gambling: Associations between self-determination theory and the transtheoretical model of change. *Journal of Addictive Diseases, 35*(1), 58–65.

Lesieur, H. R., & Blume, S. B. (1987). The South Oaks Gambling Screen (SOGS): A new instrument for the identification of pathological gamblers. *American Journal of Psychiatry, 144*, 1184–1188.

Lewis, T., Amini, F., & Lannon, R. (2000). *A general theory of love.* New York, NY: Random House.

Lin, C. Y., Broström, A., Nilsen, P., Griffiths, M. D., & Pakpour, A. H. (2017). Psychometric validation of the Persian Bergen Social Media Addiction Scale using classic test theory and Rasch models. *Journal of Behavioral Addictions, 6*(4), 620–629.

Livingston, J. D., Adams, E., Jordan, M., MacMillan, Z., & Hering, R. (2018). Primary care physicians' views about prescribing methadone to treat opioid use disorder. *Substance Use & Misuse, 53*(2), 344–353.

Lynam, D. R., Milich, R., Zimmerman, R., Novak, S. P., Logan, T. K., Martin, C. … Clayton, R. (1999). Project DARE: No effects at 10-year follow-up. *Journal of Consulting and Clinical Psychology, 67*(4), 590–593.

Marlatt, G. A. (1996). Harm reduction: Come as you are. Addictive Behaviors, *21*(6), 779–788.

McElroy, S. L., Keck, P. E., Pope, H. G., Smith, J. M. R., & Strakowski, S. M. (1994). Compulsive buying: A report of 20 cases. *Journal of Clinical Psychiatry, 55*, 242–248.

McLellan, A. T., Luborsky, L., Woody, G. E., & O'Brien, C. P. (1980). An improved diagnostic evaluation instrument for substance abuse patients: The Addiction Severity Index. *Journal of Nervous and Mental Disease, 168*(1), 26–33.

Miller, W., Rollnick, S. 2002., *Motivational Interviewing: preparing people for change.* 2nd ed. The Guilford Press, New York, N.Y.

Nadelmann, E., & LaSalle, L. (2017). Two steps forward, one step back: Current harm reduction policy and politics in the United States. *Harm Reduction Journal, 14*(1), 37.

Namratha, H., & Yeedulapally, N. R. (2018). Association of severity of alcohol dependence and occurrence of depression: A cross sectional study. *International Journal of Scientific Research, 7*(6).

Narcotics Anonymous World Services. (2016), Information about NA. Retrieved from https://www.na.org/admin/include/spaw2/uploads/pdf/pr/Info%20about%20NA_2016.pdf

Panting, H., Swift, C., Goodman, W., & Davis, C. (2018) Examining the utility of the Stages of Change model for working with offenders with learning disabilities. *Journal of Intellectual Disabilities and Offending Behaviour, 9*(2), 91–101

Peele, S. (1985). *The meaning of addiction.* San Francisco, CA: Jossey-Bass.

Peres, M. F. P., Kamei, H. H., Tobo, P. R., & Luccetti, G. (2018). Mechanisms behind religiosity and spirituality's effect on mental health, quality of life and well-being. *Journal of Religion & Health, 57*(5), 1842–1855.

Prochaska, J. O., Norcross, J. C., & DiClemete, C. C. (1994). *Changing for good: The revolutionary program that explains the six stages of change and teaches you how to free yourself from bad habits.* New York, NY: William Morrow.

Ramnath, R. D. (2004). *The assessment of online usage: From healthy use to online dependence* (Doctoral dissertation). Carlos Albizu University, Miami, FL.

Redcay, A., & Simonetti, C. (2018). Criteria for love and relationship addiction: Distinguishing love addiction from other substance and behavioral addictions. *Sexual Addiction & Compulsivity, 25*(1), 80–95.

Refuge Recovery. (2018). Retrieved from https://refugerecovery.org/about

Salem, A. A. M., Almenaye, N. S., & Andreassen, C. S. (2016). A psychometric evaluation of Bergen Facebook Addiction Scale (BFAS) of university students. *International Journal of Psychology and Behavioral Sciences, 6*(5), 199–205.

Saunders, J., Aasland, O., Babor, T., de la Fuente, J., & Grant, M. (1993). Development of the Alcohol Use Disorders Identification Test (AUDIT): WHO collaborative project on early detection of persons with harmful alcohol consumption-II. *Addiction, 88*(6), 791–804.

Segal, Z. V., Williams, M., & Teasdale, J. D. (2013). *Mindfulness-based cognitive therapy for depression* (2nd ed.). New York, NY: Guilford Press.

Selzer, M. L. (1971). The Michigan Alcoholism Screening Test: The quest for a new diagnostic instrument. *American Journal of Psychiatry, 127*, 1653–1658.

Shensa, A., Escobar-Viera, C. G., Sidani, J. E., Bowman, N. D., Marshal, M. P., & Primack, B. A. (2017). Problematic social media use and depressive symptoms among U.S. young adults: A nationally representative study. *Social Science & Medicine, 182*, 150–157.

SMART Recovery. (2018). SMART Recovery overview. Retrieved from https://www .smartrecovery.org/professionals/?_ga=2.212674900.1326912912.1539737516-604164412.1539737516

SMART Recovery. (2016) 2016 Annual Report. Retrieved from https://www.smartrecovery.org/wp-content/uploads/2018/02/2016-Annual-Report-1.pdf

Smith, A., & Anderson, M. (2018, March 1). Social media use in 2018: A majority of Americans use Facebook and YouTube, but young adults are especially heavy users of Snapchat and Instagram. Retrieved from http://www.pewinternet. org/2018/03/01/social-media-use-in-2018/

Smith, J. C., Hyman, S. M., Andres-Hyman, R. C., Ruiz, J. J., & Davidson, L. (2016, September 1). Applying recovery principles to the treatment of trauma. *Professional Psychology: Research and Practice*. Advance online publication.

Spijkerman, M. P. J., Pots, W. T. M., & Bohlmeijer, E. T. (2016). Effectiveness of online mindfulness-based interventions in improving mental health: A review and meta-analysis of randomised controlled trials. *Clinical Psychology Review, 45*, 102–114.

Starr, H. L., Bermak, J., Mao, L., Rodriguez, S., & Alphs, L. (2018). Comparison of long-acting and oral antipsychotic treatment effects in patients with schizophrenia, comorbid substance abuse, and a history of recent incarceration: An exploratory analysis of the PRIDE study. *Schizophrenia Research, 194*, 39–46.

Sternberg, R. J. (1988). *The triangle of love: Intimacy, passion, commitment.* New York, NY: Basic Books.

Straussner, S. L. A. (2014). *Clinical work with substance-abusing clients.* New York, NY: Guilford Press.Substance Abuse and Mental Health Services Administration, (SAMHSA). "National Survey on Drug Use and Health." *National Center for Biotechnology Information*, U.S. National Library of Medicine, 2014, www. ncbi.nlm.nih.gov/books/NBK519735/.

Tarter, R. (1990). Evaluation and treatment of adolescent substance abuse: A decision tree method. *American Journal of Drug and Alcohol Abuse, 16*, 1–46.

Terry, A., Szabo, A., & Griffiths, M. (2004). The exercise addiction inventory: A new brief screening tool. *Addiction Research and Theory, 12*(5), 488–499.

Trull, T. J., Freeman, L. K., Vebares, T. J., Choate, A. M., Helle, A. C., & Wycoff, A. M. (2018). Borderline personality disorder and substance use disorders: An updated review. *Borderline Personality Disorder and Emotion Dysregulation, 5*(15).

Twerski, A. J. (1997). *Addictive thinking: Understanding self-deception.* Center City, MN: Hazelden.

Verhulst, B., Neale, M. C., & Kendler, K. S. (2015). The heritability of alcohol use disorders: A meta-analysis of twin and adoption studies. *Psychological Medicine, 45*, 1061–1072.

Watkins, T. R., Lewellen, A., & Barrett, M. C. (2001). *Dual diagnosis: An integrated approach to treatment.* Thousand Oaks, CA: Sage.

Wegman, M. P., Altice, F. L., Kaur, S., Rajandaran, V., Osornprasop, S., Wilson, D., … Kamarulzaman, A. (2017). Relapse to opioid use in opioid-dependent individuals released from compulsory drug detention centres compared with those from voluntary methadone treatment centres in Malaysia: A two-arm, prospective observational study. *Lancet Global Health, 5*(2), e198–e207.

Werner, E., & Brendtro, L. (2012). Risk, resilience, and recovery. *Reclaiming Children & Youth, 21*(1), 18–22

Worden, W. J. (1991). *Grief counseling and grief therapy.* New York, NY: Springer.

Wurmser, L. (1974). Psychoanalytic considerations of the etiology of compulsive drug use. *Journal of the American Psychoanalytic Association, 22*(4), 820–843.

Yalom, I., (2002). *The gift of therapy.* New York, NY: Harper-Collins.

Young, K. S. (1996). Internet addiction: The emergence of a new clinical disorder. *CyberPsychology and Behavior, 1*(3), 237–244.

Young, K. S. (1997, August). *What makes the Internet addictive: Potential explanations for pathological Internet use.* Paper presented at the 105th annual conference of the American Psychological Association, Chicago, IL.

Young, K. (2015). The evolution of Internet addiction disorder. In C. Montag & M Reuter (Eds.), *Internet addiction* (pp. 3–17). Springer, Cham.

Ramnath Online Usage Inventory

The following statements are related to your Internet use. For each question, please circle the appropriate number that indicates your level of agreement to each statement, ranging from Strongly Agree to Strongly Disagree.

Does Not Apply	Strongly Disagree	Somewhat Disagree	Neutral	Somewhat Agree	Strongly Agree
0	1	2	3	4	5

1. The Internet Is The Only Place I Can Be Myself.   0 1 2 3 4 5

2. I Am Not Complete Without Access To The Internet.   0 1 2 3 4 5

3. I Communicate More With Family/Friends Since I Started Using The Internet.   0 1 2 3 4 5

4. I Have Gone To Sleep Later Than Usual Because I Was Online.   0 1 2 3 4 5

5. I Get A Rush From Having Multiple Online Sex Partners.   0 1 2 3 4 5

6. Since I Got The Internet, I Watch Less TV.   0 1 2 3 4 5

7. I Don't Check My E-Mail For Long Periods Of Time.   0 1 2 3 4 5

8. I Would Rather Send An E-Card Than A Real Card.   0 1 2 3 4 5

9. When I'm Offline I Think Of What I Want To Do Next On The Internet.   0 1 2 3 4 5

10. When I Log On, I Don't Usually Plan To Visit Sex-Related Websites.   0 1 2 3 4 5

11. When I Log On, I Don't Usually Plan To Play An Interactive Game.   0 1 2 3 4 5

12. I Don't Like To Compete Against Other People.   0 1 2 3 4 5

13. Whenever An Online Game Ends, I Don't Invite The Person For A Rematch.   0 1 2 3 4 5

14. I Have Engaged In Online Sex With People   0   1   2   3   4   5
    Who Would Not Have Given Me The Time
    Of Day In Person.

15. I Feel Safer Exchanging Money On A Secure   0   1   2   3   4   5
    Online Site Versus In Person.

16. I Get Excited When I Receive An Invitation   0   1   2   3   4   5
    To Play An Online Game.

17. I Have Never Ended An In-Person   0   1   2   3   4   5
    Relationship So I Can Begin A New
    Online Relationship.

18. I Find It Hard To Resist The Urge To Go   0   1   2   3   4   5
    Online At Work.

19. Since I Got The Internet, My Life   0   1   2   3   4   5
    Has Improved.

20. Each Time I Go Online, I Seem To Stay On   0   1   2   3   4   5
    Longer Than Expected.

21. I Get A Rush From Playing Against Someone   0   1   2   3   4   5
    I Don't Even Know.

22. When I Go Online, I Don't Usually Plan To   0   0   1   2   3   4
    Search For Information.

23. I Am More Sexually Confident As A Result   0   1   2   3   4   5
    Of My Online Sexual Experiences.

24. I Fulfill My Sexual Fantasies Online.   0   1   2   3   4   5

25. The People I Meet In Chat Rooms Are More   0   1   2   3   4   5
    Sincere Than In Person.

26. I Believe The Internet Is A Safer Place Than   0   1   2   3   4   5
    Real Life.

27. I Go Out As Often As I Did Before I Got   0   1   2   3   4   5
     The Internet.

28. I Find Myself Doing Things On The Internet   0   1   2   3   4   5
     That I Never Thought I Would Do.

29. I Get Bored Easily When I'm Not Online.   0   1   2   3   4   5

30. I Get Most Of My Information Online.   0   1   2   3   4   5

31. I Feel Like I Know So Much More After Each   0   1   2   3   4   5
     Use Of The Internet.

32. I Am Much More Relaxed And Focused   0   1   2   3   4   5
     When I Play A Person Online Versus
     In Person.

33. I Spend The Majority Of My Time Online   0   1   2   3   4   5
     Playing Interactive Games.

34. I Never/Rarely Visit Travel Websites If I   0   1   2   3   4   5
     Don't Plan On Traveling.

35. I Enjoy Visiting Voyeuristic Sex Websites.   0   1   2   3   4   5

36. I Spend The Majority Of My Time Online   0   1   2   3   4   5
     Surfing And Searching For Information.

37. My Holiday Shopping Is A Lot Easier Since I   0   1   2   3   4   5
     Started Buying Gifts From The Internet.

38. I Have Never Changed A Job Or Class Sched-   0   1   2   3   4   5
     ule To Accommodate My Internet Use.

39. I Have Never Dated Online.   0   1   2   3   4   5

40. I Become Hostile Toward Anyone Who Criti-   0   1   2   3   4   5
     cizes The Internet.

41. The Best Bargains Are In Online Auctions   0   1   2   3   4   5
     Like Ebay.

42. I Prefer Communicating To Friends Via   0   1   2   3   4   5
    E-Mail/Instant Messaging Versus Phone Or
    In Person.

43. I Spend The Majority Of My Time Online   0   1   2   3   4   5
    Spending, Trading, Or Betting Money.

44. I Like The Internet Because It Is Like One   0   1   2   3   4   5
    Big Encyclopedia.

45. I Enjoy Online Role-Play Games Like Multi   0   1   2   3   4   5
    User Dungeons Or Dungeons And Dragons.

46. I Am Not Ashamed Of My Sexual   0   1   2   3   4   5
    Behavior Online.

47. I Feel Anxious To Return From Home/School   0   1   2   3   4   5
    So I Can Go Online.

48. I Have Been Late For School/Work Because   0   1   2   3   4   5
    Of My Online Use.

49. I Feel A Rush Of Adrenaline Seconds Before   0   1   2   3   4   5
    An Online Connection Is Established.

50. I Like To Research Products I Don't Even   0   1   2   3   4   5
    Plan On Buying.

51. I Sometimes Feel Guilty About My   0   1   2   3   4   5
    Internet Use.

52. If You Don't Have Internet Access, You Are   0   1   2   3   4   5
    Out Of Touch With Current Events.

53. When I'm Offline, I Think About When I   0   1   2   3   4   5
    Can Go Online Again.

54. I'd Much Rather Buy Books At A Bookstore   0   1   2   3   4   5
    Than Online (e.g., Amazon.com).

55.	I Don't Stay On One Website Too Long Because I Like To Keep Looking Around For Different Information.	0	1	2	3	4	5
56.	It's More Satisfying Playing Sports With Others Outdoors Than Online.	0	1	2	3	4	5
57.	I Have Missed A Meal Because I'd Rather Be Online.	0	1	2	3	4	5
58.	My Grades/Quality Of Work Have Suffered Since I Got The Internet.	0	1	2	3	4	5
59.	I Have No Significant Relationships Online.	0	1	2	3	4	5
60.	I Would Not Care If My Online Connection Was Slow.	0	1	2	3	4	5
61.	When Someone Calls Me, I Can Leave My Computer Immediately.	0	1	2	3	4	5
62.	When I'm Offline, I Get Easily Distracted; When I'm Online, I Can Really Focus.	0	1	2	3	4	5
63.	I Feel Safe In Expressing Myself Sexually Online.	0	1	2	3	4	5
64.	I Am In Credit Card Debt As A Result Of My Online Spending.	0	1	2	3	4	5
65.	The Only Games I Play Are Against The Computer, Not Against Other Online People.	0	1	2	3	4	5
66.	When I'm Online, I'm In A "Zone."	0	1	2	3	4	5
67.	My Online Relationships Are More Satisfying Than In-Person Ones.	0	1	2	3	4	5
68.	I Think The Internet Is Overrated.	0	1	2	3	4	5

69. I Like To Enter Keywords Just To See How Many Search Results It Returns.   0 1 2 3 4 5

70. When I'm Offline, I Get Excited When I Think Of How Great I Feel When I'm Online.   0 1 2 3 4 5

71. I Have Resisted The Urge To Use The Bathroom To Remain Online.   0 1 2 3 4 5

72. I Would Rather Play My Video Games Than Online Games.   0 1 2 3 4 5

73. I Get Excited When I Enter Online Sex Groups.   0 1 2 3 4 5

74. When I Log On, I Don't Usually Plan To Communicate With Others.   0 1 2 3 4 5

75. Just Knowing I Have Access To The Internet Gives Me A Feeling Of Empowerment.   0 1 2 3 4 5

76. I Have Fun Doing Information Searches On All The People I Know.   0 1 2 3 4 5

77. I Get Frustrated When Someone Interrupts Me While I'm Online.   0 1 2 3 4 5

78. Once I Start Playing A Game Online I Don't Want It To End.   0 1 2 3 4 5

79. I Have Never Ignored Responsibilities Because Of My Internet Use.   0 1 2 3 4 5

80. I Don't Feel Jealous When Someone Else Is Online Instead Of Me.   0 1 2 3 4 5

81. I Spend The Majority Of Time Online Communicating With Others.   0 1 2 3 4 5

82. I Don't Make Online Purchases.   0 1 2 3 4 5

83.	I Hide My Online Spending From My Parents Or Significant Other.	0	1	2	3	4	5
84.	I Feel Left Out And Sad When I Can't Access The Internet.	0	1	2	3	4	5
85.	The Internet Is More Entertaining Than TV Or Radio.	0	1	2	3	4	5
86.	I Am More Open And Honest With People Online.	0	1	2	3	4	5
87.	I Like To Bet On Fantasy Sports.	0	1	2	3	4	5
88.	I Much Prefer Buying Clothes In Stores Than Online.	0	1	2	3	4	5
89.	I Have Never Downloaded Pornographic Images From The Internet.	0	1	2	3	4	5
90.	I Spend The Majority Of My Time Online In Sex-Related Websites.	0	1	2	3	4	5
91.	I Don't Get Intimidated When I Play Someone Online Like I Would In Person.	0	1	2	3	4	5
92.	I Don't Always Go Online When I Have A Chance.	0	1	2	3	4	5
93.	I Would Rather Meet People First Online Than In Person.	0	1	2	3	4	5
94.	The Best Conversations I've Had Were In Chat Rooms/News Groups/Music Groups.	0	1	2	3	4	5
95.	When I'm In A "Zone" I Feel Euphoric.	0	1	2	3	4	5
96.	I Do My Stock Trading Online.	0	1	2	3	4	5
97.	I Have Never Participated In Online Gambling.	0	1	2	3	4	5

98.   When I Go Online, I Only Visit One Or   0 1 2 3 4 5
       Two Sites.

99.   I Avoid People Who Discourage My   0 1 2 3 4 5
       Internet Use.

100. When I Go Online, I Don't Usually Plan To   0 1 2 3 4 5
       Spend Money.

101. I Prefer Online Sexual Experiences To   0 1 2 3 4 5
       Real-Life Ones.

102. I Like Buying My Groceries Online.   0 1 2 3 4 5

103. Each Time I Log On, I Rarely Do More Than   0 1 2 3 4 5
       One Search.

104. I Think Online Sex Is A Waste Of Time.   0 1 2 3 4 5

12-Step Meeting Assignment

This assignment is to attend a 12-step meeting and discuss your reaction to it. Please answer the following questions to help with the discussion:

1. Where was the meeting?
2. What day and time was it?
3. What kind of meeting did you attend (AA, NA, CA, etc.)?
4. What type of meeting was it (open, closed, speaker, step, etc.)?
5. Did you enjoy the meeting? Did you get anything out of it? Could you relate to anyone at the meeting or to anything that was said?
6. If you are attending meetings regularly, are you satisfied with your experience? Is there anything you can do to make more of this experience?

Reasons Relationships in Early Recovery Are Ill Advised

1. Takes the focus off of recovery.
2. Takes the focus off of yourself.
3. Increases the potential for relapse due to emotional intensity.
4. Too much potential for underlying issues, projections, and complexes to be creating the attraction.
5. Low self-esteem and the bargaining process of relationships.
6. Strong likelihood of outgrowing the relationship quickly.
7. You do not really know yourself yet.
8. You do not know what love is yet.
9. Likely acting on, "I want what I want when I want it".
10. In light of advice to the contrary, if you decide to enter a relationship, you are working your own program. This is an addictive behavior.

Printed in the USA
CPSIA information can be obtained
at www.ICGtesting.com
LVHW011932171023
761385LV00014B/44